Dearest Coz

A Very Happy
Birthday

With our love
Minna and Jamie

14th July 2002

$\mathcal{S}$ The $\mathcal{S}$ALMON Cook

99 Ways with Salmon

~

Hannah Sykes

The Crowood Press

First published in 1994 by
The Crowood Press Ltd
Ramsbury, Marlborough
Wiltshire SN8 2HR

British Library Cataloguing-in-Publication Data

A catalogue record for this book is available from the British Library.

ISBN 1 85223 842 9

Dedication
To Jonny and Alicia

Picture Credits
Line-drawings by David Haig-Thomas.
Diagrams by Claire Upsdale-Jones.

Typeset by Phoenix Typesetting, Ilkley, West Yorkshire.
Printed and bound in Great Britain by Hazell Books Ltd.
A member of The British Printing Company Ltd.

Acknowledgements
My thanks to Leiths School of Food and Wine where I trained: a more
thorough grounding in the art of cooking would be hard to gain in the
time I was there. All my basic techniques and some of my ideas come
from their teachings and may appear familiar to them for this reason.

I would also thank my heroine, Jane Grigson. Since leaving Leiths,
she has been the single greatest influence on my cooking style and will
probably remain so as her general attitudes to cooking have always
inspired me enormously.

Contents

AUTHOR'S NOTE

This book was written with both wild and farmed salmon in mind. I hope this is clearly reflected in the variety of recipes. Some purely enhance and celebrate the qualities of this king of fishes, while others use imaginative combinations and techniques that show just how versatile it can be.

I have tried to use ingredients that are easy to find in the high street and supermarket, avoiding things like ripe mangoes! Metric and imperial measurements are fully interchangeable. Where I have been vague with quantities – 'a bunch of chives', for example – I have intended that it should be left to personal tastes, availability, or financial constraints.

INTRODUCTION

It is upsetting to see cod, haddock and plaice being priced out of every-day reach for no better reason than overfishing. However, all is not lost because the once seasonal delicacy, salmon, is now farmed cleanly and efficiently, making available a wonderful fish at an affordable price. Salmon enjoyed a meteoric rise in popularity throughout the 1980s, emerging in the 1990s as a healthy, versatile and nutritious favourite.

THE SALMON'S PROPERTIES

In the UK, wild salmon are in season between the months of February and August and are superior both in texture and taste to their farmed cousins. Salmon has a firm textured flesh and a fine flavour that is not complicated by excessive boniness. It is an oily fish, which means it can take more varied methods of cooking than white fish, which stores its fat purely in the liver.

The one point that people often overlook in the cooking of salmon is the length of time it takes. Overcooked salmon is a joyless experience: dry, tasteless and tough; it should be avoided at all costs. With a little care, however, salmon will respond admirably and never cease to be a special treat. In my opinion it is the most adaptable of all our fishes.

When salmon is caught and cooked very fresh, a white creamy substance known as the curd will be seen between the flakes. Some people feel this is rather indigestible, in which case the fish can be left uncooked for a couple of days, during which time the curd will subside, making the flesh richer though less delicious in flavour.

NUTRITIONAL VALUES

Fish are high in polyunsaturated fat, which is less bad for our arteries than the saturated fats found in meats and dairy products. Oily fish such as salmon are also an excellent source of omega 3 polyunsaturates – a substance that has been proven to help reduce the risk of heart disease and can prevent post-surgical complications with the heart as well. Other benefits include the reduction of high blood pressure and relief from complaints as varied as arthritis, eczema, and asthma.

For those who watch their calorie intake: 100g (3½oz) of steamed salmon has 160 Kcalories and 100g (3½oz) of smoked salmon only 142. This compares favourably with chicken: when poached the same quantity will yield 183 Kcal.

PREPARING SALMON

Initial Preparation

The first thing to do is to gut the fish. On a very fresh fish the innards smell of nothing more than the sea so the squeamish need not fear! Insert a very sharp knife into the soft belly of the fish near the head. With a sawing motion, cut down the belly until you reach the fish's vent, about two-thirds of the way down. Draw the insides out and wash the salmon thoroughly, ensuring that all the blood from the spine has been removed (use a teaspoon to help scrape this away). Then, cut the gills out from inside the cavity using poultry shears.

If your chosen recipe requires that you leave the skin on, the large 'dry' scales need to be removed. Place the fish in a large plastic bag; a carrier bag is ideal. Hold on to the tail and drag a heavy knife up the length of the salmon over and over again, and watch the scales fly off! This is a horrible and messy job. If you have bought your fish from a fishmonger get him to do it: he has what looks like a curry comb for horses to help him, and also the mess will be in his shop and not in your kitchen!

Salmon can be further prepared by: cutting it into steaks; filleting it, leaving two long sides of boneless flesh, which can then be skinned; slicing it into minute steaks or escalopes; stuffing and cooking it whole, with or without the skeleton in.

Cutting Steaks

A steak is cut straight through the fish, leaving a cross-section of flesh with the spine in the centre. As a guide, an average 170g (6oz) steak is about 2.5cm (1in) thick.

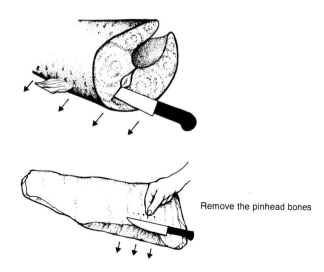

Filleting

Remove the pinhead bones

Filleting

Lay a whole salmon on a board with its back to you and cut off the head and tail. Then, inserting your knife next to the spine, draw it towards you, through the flesh and out through the skin on the fish's back, using the bones to guide and keep you straight. Repeat this motion right down the upper portion of the body. Go back to your starting point where the head was and repeat on the thinner 'belly' fillet. Having removed the first side, turn the fish over and repeat the process. Finally, remove the 'pin-head' bones with tweezers or strong fingers from the centre of the fillets and cut away the pale, tough stomach lining.

Skinning

Lay a fillet skin side down, with the tail end towards you. Grip the very tip of the tail with your fingers, clamping it to the board (a pinch of salt can help here). Insert the knife blade into the flesh (but not through the skin) just in front of your fingers, at right angles to the fish. Using a sideways sawing movement push the knife slowly away towards the thick end; the fillet will magically lift and curl ahead of the knife blade. Alternatively you can keep the knife held still, at 45 degrees, and move the tail behind the knife blade from side to side, pulling the fish's skin

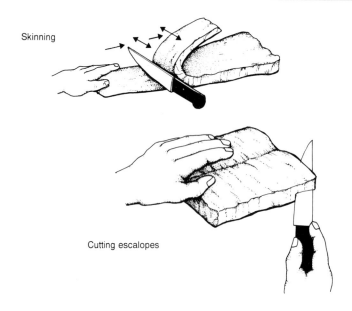

Skinning

Cutting escalopes

slowly towards you. If the fillet was previously frozen you can simply peel the skin off with your fingers.

Escalopes

Take a filleted and skinned piece of salmon (340g/12oz makes two). Lay it skinned side down. With a very sharp knife, gently start cutting through the fillet horizontally. You can make large escalopes of 170g (6oz) that serve one, or smaller ones to serve two or three to each diner.

Boning a Whole Fish

To stuff a whole fish, gut and remove the gills and then de-scale as described above. Scrape any blood from the backbone as this will impart a bitter taint to the cooked flesh.

If you wish to present a fully boned stuffed fish then lengthen the cavity opening from the head right down to the tail. Slide a sharp knife round both sides of the spine, starting from the tail end and working upwards until you reach the obtrusive rib bones. Ease these bones away from the flesh using your fingers or a knife blade. Then simply snip through the spine with poultry shears as high up and as low down as possible, and ease it away from the fish. Rub your fingers down each side

Boning a whole fish

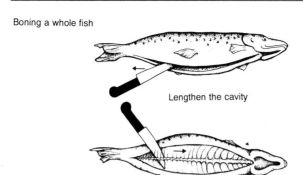

Lengthen the cavity

Slide a sharp knife around both sides of the spine

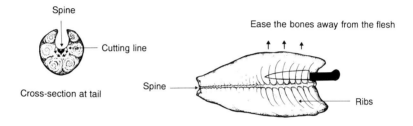

Spine

Cutting line

Cross-section at tail

Ease the bones away from the flesh

Spine

Cross-section at tail

Ribs

to ensure that all bones have been removed.

Do not forget that your fishmonger is highly skilled and willing to help, whether he works for a supermarket or an independent shop. If you don't feel up to tackling the fish yourself, ask for his help.

Preparing a Fish for the Freezer

If you are lucky enough to catch, or be given a salmon, but cannot eat it immediately then gut it, wrap it really well to prevent any air from damaging it and freeze it whole, or cut into individual portions. Supermarkets sometimes sell salmon whole on special offer, and if you have a deep freeze it is a good idea to buy such a fish and keep it frozen either whole or cut into individual servings. For example, a 2.7kg (6lb) salmon will yield seven 170g (6oz) steaks, which are 2.5cm (1in) thick. It will also give two 170g (6oz) tail fillets, and if you then scrape the flesh from the tail bones and from the head it will give a further 110g (4oz) of flesh, perfect for recipes such as the salmon cutlets on page 63. Do not rinse the portions as you will be washing away some of the flavour; wrap them in cling film and freeze down as quickly as possible.

COOKING TIMES

In a Fish Kettle

To be eaten cold   Bring slowly to a simmer. If it is a large fish simmer for 3 minutes before removing from the heat and leaving until cold. For a smaller fish (under 3.2kg/7lb) bring to a simmer and remove immediately from the heat, then leave until cold.

To be eaten hot   Allow 10 minutes for a fish under 3.2kg (7lb) and 15 minutes for a larger one. After this add 9 minutes to the kilo (4 minutes to the pound).
   Another way is to calculate the time according to the depth of girth of your salmon. Bring to a simmer slowly, then allow 3 minutes per centimetre (7½ minutes per inch). Turn the heat off and leave for a further 15 minutes before serving.

In Foil

To serve cold   If your fish is too large to fit flat on a baking tray, there are two alternative methods:

1.   Cut into two pieces, wrap separately in foil, weigh individually, and bake for 44 minutes to the kilo (20 minutes to the pound) at 170°C/325°F/Gas Mark 3. Reassemble when cold and hide the join under your decoration.
2.   Curl the fish round, making it sit up on its belly, then bake as before. The recipe on page 13 for a whole baked fish suggests flavourings to add.

To serve hot   Bake with the seasonings suggested on page 21. For a fish under 3.2kg (7lb), bake for 44 minutes to the kilo (20 minutes to the pound) at 170°C/325°F/Gas Mark 3. For larger fish add an extra 8 minutes to the cooking time.

STOCK

Salmon is not ideal for making fish stock because the carcass can be both oily and bloody. However if you are prepared to skim the fat or not to use the skin this difficulty can be averted. Bloodiness in the stock will give a bitter taint. Cut the gills out of the head if you are using this. If these points are remembered it will make a richly flavoured stock.

A light chicken or veal stock can be substituted for any fish stock required in recipes here.

SERVING SALMON

Salmon skin is fatty and quite thick so unless the fish is grilled or fried to make the skin crisp, it is better to remove it altogether. For a fish that will be eaten cold, the skin should be removed when just warm. This way, it is easy to remove and the fish does not dry out through loss of steam. If serving the salmon hot, the skin only takes a second to remove using a knife and fork. Remove all that is possible without turning the fish over.

If presenting a whole hot fish to your guests, one of the beauties of salmon is that the flesh parts easily from the bones and remains relatively in one piece, making it easy to serve. Split the two upper fillets with a knife and slide the upper thick fillet off. It will feed one person more than the lower, thinner fillet which is slightly harder to manage. When the uppermost side of the fish has been served, snip the spine at head and tail, peel away and serve the underside fillets, leaving the skin on the plate.

CHAPTER 1

WHOLE FISH

Poaching a Whole Fish

The method described here is a fool-proof way to tackle what is often considered a nerve-wracking process.

1 whole salmon, cleaned and gutted
cold court bouillon (see page 124), sufficient to cover the fish

To eat cold

1   Put the fish into a fish kettle. Pour the cold court bouillon over the fish and set on the heat. Bring to the boil, quite slowly; then lower the heat immediately to a gentle simmer.

2   If the fish is over 3.2kg (7lb), cook for 3 minutes before removing from the heat; if under 3.2kg (7lb), remove from the heat immediately the stock boils. Once removed from the heat, leave the fish in the stock to get completely cold. Your fish will then be cooked to perfection. If you haven't got the time to wait for it to become completely cold in the stock, cook as instructed below for eating hot; then remove from the stock, cover with foil and allow to cool.

To eat hot

1   Follow step 1 above.

2   Simmer for 10 minutes, then 9 minutes to the kilo (4 minutes to the pound). If the fish is over 3.2kg (7lb), simmer for 15 minutes before calculating the amount by weight.

3   Remove from the stock and skin.

Serving suggestion: Serve with a sauce of your choice, and/or a cucumber and dill salad dressed with vinaigrette.

Baking a Whole Fish

In many ways baking is preferable to poaching: not only do you remove the need for a specialist fish kettle, but all nutrients are kept within the fish instead of leaching into the water.

1 whole salmon, cleaned and gutted   *parsley stalks*
1 stick celery   *3 slices of lemon*
1 bay leaf   *60ml/2fl oz white wine*
1 sprig thyme   *seasoning*

Pre-heat oven to 170°C/325°F/Gas Mark 3.

---

1   Scrape any blood from the spine using a teaspoon. Wipe the fish out with a damp clean cloth.

---

2   Find the largest baking tray or roasting tin you possess (but check that it will go in the oven!). Line the tray with tin foil, allowing a generous overlap on both sides.

---

3   Lay the fish on the foil. If it is too big for the tray sit it up slightly on its belly, pulling the head and tail round.

---

4   Season the inside of the fish liberally. Place the other ingredients in the cavity, pour over the wine, and then wrap the fish carefully in the foil. The foil should not allow any steam to escape.

---

5   Bake for 44 minutes to the kilo (20 minutes to the pound). If the fish is larger than 3.2kg (7lb), allow an extra 10 minutes on the cooking time.

---

6   When cooked, the flesh should just part from the bones. Unwrap and serve with a sauce, or leave until just warm before skinning and decorating the fish as described on pages 16–17.

Serving suggestion: Wrapped in foil, the salmon could be cooked on the barbecue. Turn regularly, and allow between 1 and 2 hours, depending on the size of the fish and the barbecue.

Salmon Stuffed and Baked

Serves 5

This is a good, basic, lemony stuffing, which you could elaborate on or use for stuffing another type of fish; the instructions can also serve as a guideline for stuffing a salmon with your own favourite recipe. You may prefer to bone the salmon, in which case simply follow the instructions on page 9. If you wish to stuff the fish as it is – with the skeleton still intact – wash the inside thoroughly, making sure that any blood on the spine has been scraped away with a teaspoon.

1 whole salmon (1.35kg/3lb)
170g/6oz butter
55ml/2fl oz white wine
salt and pepper
juice of 1 lemon

For the stuffing:
2 small slices crustless bread, soaked
* in milk*
55g/2oz mushrooms, sliced
2 anchovy fillets, finely chopped
1 hard-boiled egg, chopped
grated rind of 1 lemon
salt and pepper

Pre-heat oven to 190°C/375°F/Gas Mark 5.

1   Squeeze the excess milk from the bread. Mash with a fork, then stir in the anchovy fillets, mushrooms, egg, and the grated lemon rind. Season well.

2   Stuff the cavity with the bread mixture, then knit the belly flaps together with cocktail sticks, or tie in several places with string. (If the fish has not been boned, the cavity will be smaller, which means that you will have some stuffing left over; shape this remainder into balls and bake around the salmon.)

3   Place in a baking dish and spread liberally with some of the butter. Pour the wine around it and season well. Cover with foil and bake for 50 minutes. (If the fish is larger than 1.35kg (3lb), bake for 44 minutes to the kilogram (20 minutes to the pound).

4   Just before the fish is cooked, squeeze the lemon juice into a pan. Add the remaining butter; melt and boil up for a second to amalgamate. Pour over the fish and return to the oven for a further 10 minutes.

5   Drain the fish juices into a sauce-boat. Skin the salmon, and serve with a simple vegetable, such as broccoli.

Salmon Baked with Cucumber

Serves 4

Cucumber is a perfect foil for salmon: delicate in flavour, it has a tender bite that is different yet in keeping with the firm flakes of the fish.

1 whole salmon (1.35kg/3lb)
290ml/10fl oz double cream
2 bay leaves
1 cucumber
85g/3oz butter
juice of 1 lemon
salt and pepper

Pre-heat oven to 180°C/350°F/Gas Mark 4.

Note: For a different-sized fish, allow 44 minutes to the kilogram or 20 minutes to the pound.

---

1   Clean the fish. Place the bay leaves in the cavity, season well, rub the butter all over, and lay it in a baking dish.

---

2   Pour the cream around, not on to, the fish.

---

3   Cover the dish with foil or paper and bake for 30 minutes. (Remember that if the dish is particularly heavy, the cooking times may need to be increased.)

---

4   Peel and cube the cucumber. Sprinkle with salt and leave to drain in a sieve.

---

5   Add cucumber to the salmon, along with the lemon juice. Replace in the oven, this time without a covering, and bake for a further 30 minutes.

---

6   Remove the fish to a serving dish and skin. Season the cucumber cream sauce, pour over the salmon, and serve.

Serving suggestion: The interesting buttery bitterness of endive goes well with this; as does spinach.

Decorating a Whole Fish in the Traditional Way

Everyone has a different idea about how to decorate a fish, and you should let your imagination have a free rein. However, these guidelines will be useful for those with little confidence. Traditionally, the head and tail of a whole decorated salmon are left on and the fish left on the bone, but some who prefer not to be confronted by a baleful eye will wish to dispense with the head. Whilst leaving the skeleton intact makes for a better-shaped cold fish, it also makes it more difficult to serve.

1 cold salmon, poached or baked as described on pages 12–13

For the decoration:
*300ml/10fl oz mayonnaise, made with extra oil to make it stiffer than usual (*see page 120*)*
1 small cucumber
watercress
½ lemon
1 olive
salt

1   If you wish to remove the head, this should be done before cooking. Using a strong, sharp knife cut straight across the neck. If you are poaching the salmon, rather than baking it, include the severed head (having first removed the gills) in the stock. If you wish to remove the tail as well, do so after cooking.

2   If you are leaving the head and tail intact, take a sharp knife and cut a 'V' shape in the skin of the salmon: start at the back of the head, draw to a point level with the eye, then direct the knife back out to the body side of the fin (leaving the wobbly, tough 'collar bone'). Trim the tail into a tidier 'V' shape.

3   Carefully skin the fish down to the tail, leaving the head untouched. At the tail, again cut the skin into a tidier 'V', with the point of the 'V' facing down the fish, away from the head. Remove the pale gelled line from along the top of the salmon's back.

4   If you are going to remove the skeleton, do so now; using a sharp knife, carefully divide one side of the fish into fillets, and ease them from the bones, trying to keep them intact. With a sharp pair of scissors, cut through the spine

at the head and tail. Lift the skeleton off the lower side of the fish. Check for any bones left in the flesh. Gently scrape away the white stomach lining and the soft floor of the belly, then slide these lower two fillets off the remaining skin and replace in a similar position on the serving dish.

5 Spread the stiff mayonnaise over these fillets. Gently return the other two fillets to their place. The fish will have lost some of its shape where the gullet is no longer supported. (Don't worry if the fillets have not stayed wholly intact; use mayonnaise as glue and cucumber to hide any errors.)

6 Peel and then slice the cucumber very finely. Layer the slices up in a sieve or between inverted plates, salting as you go; leave for 20 minutes. This draws much of the excess water from them, which is necessary if the salmon is to be decorated well in advance of being served.

7 Starting at the tail, lay the cucumber slices on the fish, overlapping each by half, working up to the head, so that they resemble scales.

8 If the salmon is headless, continue the cucumber over the end. Take the washed watercress stalk by stalk, and arrange the leaves into a good tight bouquet. Holding the bunch firmly just under its head, twist and pull off the stalks. Place at the head of the fish. Repeat for the tail end if this has also been removed.

9 If the salmon's head and tail have been left intact, simply remove the eye and replace with a black olive.

10 Take thin slices from the lemon. Cut from the skin into the central core of each slice. Twist and place in a row down the lower side of the salmon.

Serving suggestion: Serve with mayonnaise thinned to a more sauce-like consistency, or with one of the cold sauces as described in Chapter 7. With such a magnificent centrepiece, keep any accompanying salads simple and classic: lettuce, cucumber salad, and a new potato vinaigrette.

Whole Salmon Chaudfroid

If the surface of your poached salmon has become damaged for some reason during cooking or skinning, this is a good way to hide mistakes. It is also a more original and, I think, polished way of presenting a whole fish. Instead of a beautiful velouté sauce, you could use gellied mayonnaise.

1 whole salmon, gutted and cleaned
cold court bouillon, or wine and
   water, sufficient to cover the fish
15g/½ oz gelatine

For the decoration:
Any of the following: dill, chervil,
anchovy fillet, quails' eggs,
mushroom or truffle.

For the sauce:
20g/¾ oz butter
20g/¾ oz flour
150ml/5fl oz milk
150ml/5fl oz fish aspic made from
the reserved stock
6 peppercorns
1 blade mace
1 bay leaf
1 slice onion
2 tablespoons double or single cream
salt and white pepper

1   Poach salmon in the stock (*see* page 12). After cooking, reserve 425ml/15fl oz of the stock and chill.

2   Remove any trace of fat from the stock and then strain carefully through a double layer of muslin or a clean tea-towel.

3   From the strained stock, make approximately 275ml (10fl oz) of fish aspic: place 4 tablespoons of the stock in a small bowl; sprinkle the gelatine over this and leave to soak in for five minutes. Heat the bowl gently in a pan of hot water. When completely melted and clear, stir in all but 150ml (5fl oz) of the strained fish stock. Cool.

4   Make the sauce. Heat the milk gently with the bay leaf, peppercorns, the blade of mace and the onion. Meanwhile, melt the butter, add the flour and cook for one minute. Strain the milk infusion on to the butter and flour and whisk until smooth. Add the 150ml (5fl oz) of stock reserved when making the aspic, and return to the heat, bring to the boil, stirring until thickened. Simmer gently for a few minutes. Stir the cream, seasoning and 150ml (5fl oz) of the fish aspic into this. Cool.

5   Skin the fish, but do not bone. Place on its serving dish. Dab gently with kitchen paper to absorb any excess moisture or grease. If you prefer the fish filleted, do so, sandwiching it back together with mayonnaise.

6   While the sauce is still cold but not yet setting, spoon carefully over the skinned portions of the fish. Let the sauce fall in a curtain; your aim is a complete and unblemished covering.

7   Replace the fish's eye with a black olive. Arrange the tiny sprigs of dill and/or chervil and the slices of truffle or mushroom, julienned pieces of anchovy fillet and slices of quail's egg over the skinned part of the fish. Keep the decoration simple for maximum effect. Chill.

8   Melt the remaining aspic (about 125ml/4fl oz), then allow to cool until it is about to jelly. Spoon very carefully over the decorated body and the unskinned head. When it has set, repeat with another layer.

Serving suggestion: Serve with mayonnaise thinned with water to a more sauce-like consistency.

Cold Salmon with Montpellier Butter

Serves 4

This can be done with either a whole salmon, a middle cut or a filleted piece.

*900g/2lb piece middle cut
  salmon
cold court bouillon, or wine
  and water, sufficient to
  cover the fish
255g/9oz Montpellier butter (see
  page 119)*

For the decoration:
*hard-boiled quail's eggs
anchovy fillets
capers
tarragon leaves
wafer-thin slices of truffle, or
  mushroom*

---

1   Poach salmon in court bouillon. Allow to cool.

---

2   Skin and fillet the salmon; slide the fillets from one side of the fish on to a serving dish.

---

3   Spread some of the softened Montpellier butter on to the fillets. Replace the fillets from the other side of the fish, and cover with two-thirds of the remaining butter. Put the last third into cling-film, roll into a sausage shape, and chill well.

---

4   Cut the chilled roll of butter into little round pats and use with the other remaining ingredients to decorate the fish in any way you like.

Serving suggestion: You could serve this with baked potatoes, to which Montpellier butter has beeen added.

CHAPTER 2

BAKED, GRILLED AND FRIED

Baked Salmon Steaks in Foil

This has to be the easiest way to cook salmon. Quick, clean, in easy portions; it is also infinitely variable. Try adding plenty of rosemary, thyme, bay, fennel, dill or marjoram. You could also experiment with seasonings: try a little French mustard, anchovy essence or some grated nutmeg.

1 salmon steak per person (each about 170g/6oz)
butter
pepper and sea salt
lemon juice

Pre-heat oven to 180°C/350°F/Gas Mark 4.

1   Cut baking foil into as many 30cm (12in) square pieces as you have steaks; spread each liberally with butter.

2   Lay a steak in the centre of each, season well, and add a squeeze of lemon. Add any chosen herb or seasoning and the butter now. Wrap the steaks up, making them airtight but still allowing a little room inside.

3   Place foil parcels on a baking tray and bake for about 15 minutes. If you are baking more than 4 parcels, pre-heat the baking sheet you are placing them on. This will ensure the salmon cooks more quickly, helping to seal in the juices.

Serving suggestion: Serve with a creamy potato dish, such as a Pommes Dauphinoise.

Grilled Salmon with Flavoured Butters

Serves 4

These butters are also delicious as a base for sandwiches, or on a grilled lamb chop or piece of fillet steak. See also the anchovy, green and garlic and lemon butters in Chapter 7.

4 salmon steaks (170g/6oz each)
110g/4oz butter
oil
salt and pepper

For the filling:
Either:
4 tablespoons finely chopped mixed
* herbs: parsley, marjoram and dill*
squeeze of lemon juice
salt and pepper

Or:
225g/8oz washed spinach leaves
pinch of grated nutmeg
squeeze of lemon juice
salt and pepper

Or:
4 teaspoons French mustard
juice of ½ lemon
salt and pepper

1   Clean the steaks and remove any loose scales. Brush with oil and season with pepper. Process the flavouring you have chosen with the butter. Place on a piece of cling-film or grease-proof paper, and fashion into a sausage shape. Chill.

2   Sprinkle the steaks with salt and place under a medium-high pre-heated grill, about 8cm (3in) from the element. Grill for 3 to 4 minutes on each side.

3   Unwrap the butter; slice into eight pieces. Place 2 on each steak and serve immediately.

Serving suggestion: A green salad and new potatoes tossed in butter make an accompaniment of calm simplicity, nothing more is necessary.

Minute Steaks with Aigrellette Sauce

Serves 4

Aigrellette sauce seems to strike just the right balance between the richness and texture of the fried salmon escalopes.

900g/2lb middle cut salmon
55g/2oz butter
seasoned flour
225ml/8fl oz Aigrellette sauce (see
*   page 121)*

---

1   Fillet and skin the salmon, leaving you with 2 thick pieces. With a sharp knife, carefully cut through the salmon horizontally, so that you end up with 4 thin escalopes (*see* pages 8–9).

---

2   Make the sauce. Set in a bowl over simmering water to heat up. This takes only a few minutes.

---

3   Melt the butter in a large frying pan. When foaming, dip 2 escalopes in seasoned flour and lay in the pan. They should be ready to turn over in 2 minutes. When they are just cooked (this may be in less than 4 minutes, depending on their thickness), keep warm in a very low oven while the next two are cooking.

---

4   Ladle the sauce over the fish, or decant into a sauce-boat for the table.

Serving suggestion: Serve with a vegetable that will embrace the Aigrellette, such as broccoli.

Salmon Steaks in Newspaper

Serves 4

This recipe can be adapted to any firm-fleshed fish, or even to a chicken or pheasant breast. Grease-proof paper is sufficient, but it is more fun to use a newspaper, especially a pink one like the *Financial Times*.

4 salmon steaks, 170g/6oz each
55g/2oz carrot julienne
55g/2oz celery julienne
55g/2oz fennel julienne
½ small onion, finely sliced
splash of white wine

55g/2oz butter
4 tablespoons double or whipping
* cream*
2 tablespoons finely chopped parsley
salt and pepper

Pre-heat oven to 200°C/400°F/Gas Mark 6.

1   Combine the four vegetables and sweat in the butter until tender.

2   Cut out 4 generous-sized circles of grease-proof paper. Place each one in the centre of 4 sheets of newspaper. Put the steaks on the grease-proof paper and season well.

3   Stir the cream, parsley and wine into the cooked julienne and divide equally between the fish.

4   Wrap each parcel carefully: first fold over the inner grease-proof paper, twisting the edges together at the top to make a Cornish pasty shape; then repeat with the outer newspaper, folding into a neat parcel.

5   Slide the parcels carefully on to a baking tray and bake for 15 minutes.

6   Leave the parcels wrapped for your guests to undo at the table. Remember to put out a large bowl for the discarded wrappings.

Serving suggestion: The balance between fish and vegetables is perfect in this recipe, so do not add more; instead try serving with plain rice – to which wild rice has been added – to mop up the creamy juices.

Salmon en Papillote

Serves 4

Some people – my parents included – think it very odd to serve paper parcels at dinner. The contents seem to set quite firmly, so for them I carefully slide them out and then pour the sauce over.

480g/1lb 2oz salmon fillet
55g/2oz butter
4 shallots
1 clove garlic
225g/8oz mushrooms
salt and pepper

2 tablespoons finely chopped dill, or
1 tablespoon finely chopped
*   tarragon*
4 tablespoons white wine
300ml/10fl oz beurre blanc (see
*   page 116)*

Pre-heat oven to 230°C/450°F/Gas Mark 8.

---

1   Finely chop the shallots, crush the garlic and sweat them in the butter until the shallots are soft and translucent. Add the sliced mushrooms, raise the heat and stir briskly. After a minute, the mushrooms will release their liquid. Continue cooking until this liquid has evaporated off. Season well, stir in the dill or tarragon, and allow to cool.

---

2   Cut 4 large circles from grease-proof paper. Lightly butter them; divide the mushroom mixture between them.

---

3   Skin the salmon and slice into 24 1cm (½in) slices. Lay 5 on each bed of mushroom. Add a tablespoon of wine to each. Twist the paper edges together to make a good seal on each parcel. Put a baking tray in a very hot oven.

---

4   Make the beurre blanc and keep warm in a double boiler, or flask.

---

5   When you are ready to eat, take the baking tray out of the oven, put the parcels on it, well spaced out, and quickly return to the oven. They should be cooked in about 5 or 6 minutes.

---

6   Either undo the parcels, or cut a hole in the top of each – whichever is quicker – and pour in some beurre blanc. Serve immediately.

Serving suggestion: Serve this with a dish of braised fennel.

Pot-Pourri Parcels

Serves 4

These were invented by my mother. You can use other types of fish; and if you wish you can even add vegetables, such as button mushrooms, to them, in which case cook first in butter until they have released their juices.

110g/4oz salmon, skinned and
   filleted
2 large or 4 small scallops
1 sole, skinned and filleted, or
   110g/4oz of other firm-fleshed fish,
   such as turbot or halibut

8 Dublin Bay prawns
lemon juice
salt and pepper
1 tablespoon finely chopped dill or
   parsley
30g/1oz butter

Pre-heat oven to 220°C/425°F/Gas Mark 7.

1   Cube the salmon. If using large scallops, halve them horizontally; cut the sole into pieces of a similar size.

2   Mix the salmon, scallops and sole with the prawns and dill or parsley. Season liberally with salt, pepper and lemon juice.

3   Butter 4 pieces of foil generously. Divide the mixture equally between the foil pieces. Draw up the sides to make little purse-shaped packages. Pinch the tops together to make a good seal.

4   Bake in a hot oven, for 15 minutes.

Serving suggestion: Serve with a more formal vegetable, such as Duchesse potato and spinach for ideal accompaniments.

Shashlik of Salmon

Serves 4

The egg and breadcrumb coating helps to protect the salmon from the potentially drying effects of a hot grill. It also adds interestingly to the texture. A beurre blanc or beurre montée would be ideal to moisten and marry the flavours.

450g/1lb salmon
salt
juice of 1 lemon
55g/2oz dried breadcrumbs, made
    from 110g/4oz fresh ones

1 egg
20 button mushrooms (280g/10oz)
15g/½oz butter
55g/2oz melted butter
salt and pepper

1   Fillet and skin the salmon. Cut into 20 3cm (1in) cubes . Sprinkle with salt and the lemon juice.

2   Lightly sauté the whole mushrooms in 15g/½oz butter.

3   Dip each salmon cube into the beaten eggs and then into the breadcrumbs.

4   Thread onto 4 skewers, alternating with the mushrooms. Brush liberally with the melted butter, especially the salmon. Season well.

5   Grill the shashliks under a moderate heat until the breadcrumbs look crisp (2 or 3 minutes on each side).

Serving suggestion: Serve with a plain, fresh watercress salad.

Brochettes of Salmon and Scallops

Serves 4 as a starter; 2 as a main course

These fish 'kebabs' are marinated briefly in oil and fennel, but dill can be substituted for fennel. A few rashers of bacon, cut into squares, could also be added, although purists wouldn't approve! If serving as a starter, try serving 2 mini brochettes instead of 1 large one by cutting 30cm (12in) bamboo skewers into two.

12 small scallops, or 6 large ones	*virgin olive oil*
340g/12oz piece of salmon, skinned and filleted	*sea salt and pepper*
	15g/½ oz butter
1 tablespoon of finely chopped fennel, or dill	*1 cucumber*

1   Remove the corals from the scallops. If the scallops are large, slice them in half horizontally.

2   Cube the salmon into an equal number of pieces. Place in a bowl with the scallops, season with pepper and the fennel, and pour over a couple of tablespoons of oil. Mix well and leave to marinate for at least 20 minutes.

3   Meanwhile, peel the cucumber with a swivel-headed peeler; discard the peel. Turning the cucumber round in one hand, peel off full-length strips of the flesh, continuing until you reach the seeds. As you get nearer the centre and the cucumber becomes floppy, lay it on a flat surface and continue paring it down; discard the seed core. Salt the cucumber 'tagliatelle' and leave it to degorge for about 20 minutes.

4   Heat the grill. Make the brochettes: place the marinated salmon and scallops alternately on to skewers. Just before cooking, sprinkle with salt. (Do not use salt any earlier because it will draw precious juices out.)

5   Grill the brochettes for 10 to 12 minutes (depending on the strength of your grill); turn them half-way through the grilling time. When you turn them over, brush with the remaining marinade.

6 Half-way through the grilling, gently squeeze the water from the cucumber strips by pressing them in a clean cloth. Melt the butter in a frying pan and sauté the cucumber strips for about 3 minutes until they begin to look floppy and cooked. Season with pepper.

7 Swirl the cucumber strips around on individual plates and place the grilled brochettes on top.

Serving suggestion: If making this a main course, serve with new potatoes.

Salmon with Shallots and Mushrooms

Serves 4

Whilst baby onions and button mushrooms are a classic garnish for beef and venison stews, their flavour and texture lend themselves favourably to salmon too.

4 salmon steaks (170g/6oz each)
85g/3oz butter
290ml/10fl oz fish stock
a small wine glass white wine
8 shallots
16 button mushrooms

For the sauce:
50ml/2fl oz cooking liquid, reduced
* from the fish stock*
150ml/5fl oz double cream
2 tablespoons finely chopped chervil
* (or parsley), or 1 tablespoon*
* finely chopped tarragon*
salt and pepper

Pre-heat oven to 190°C/375°F/Gas Mark 5.

1   Heat 30g (1oz) of the butter in a frying pan; seal the steaks in the butter (a few seconds each side will suffice).

2   Transfer to an ovenproof dish and pour over the wine and stock, which should come nearly to the top of the steaks. Cover and bake for about 15 minutes.

3   Meanwhile, blanch the shallots for 4 minutes. Melt a further 30g (1oz) of the butter and sauté the mushrooms. Remove with a slotted spoon and keep warm.

4   Fry the shallots in the remaining butter until the outer skin begins to brown. Keep warm.

5   When the salmon is cooked, remove from the liquid and keep warm. Pour the cooking liquid into a saucepan and reduce down to about 50ml (2fl oz) or 4 tablespoons.

6   Stir in the cream, bring back to the boil and simmer for a few minutes until

the sauce has thickened a little. Stir in the chervil and check the seasoning.

7   Arrange the steaks on a plate with the vegetables. Pour the sauce over the fish only and serve.

Serving suggestion: French beans and mashed potato complement the sturdy feel of this dish.

D.H.T.

Pan-Fried Salmon with Cream

Serves 4

This is another classic way to cook tender cuts of meat or fish, in which the colour and some of the flavour in the sauce comes from the pan juices. If preferred, the cream can be exchanged for soured cream.

*4 salmon steaks (170g/6oz each), or
  675g/1lb 8oz salmon fillet,
  skinned and cut into 4 pieces
55g/2oz butter
1 teaspoon chopped thyme*

For the cream sauce:
*2 shallots, finely chopped
½ wine glass white wine
1 wine glass fish stock
4 tablespoons double cream
salt and pepper*
Optional: *1 teaspoon parsley,
  chopped*

1   Fry the salmon gently in a pan with the butter, salt, pepper and thyme. This will take about 5 minutes on each side for steaks, 3 minutes for fillets. Remove from the pan and keep warm.

2   Finely chop the shallots and cook until soft in the fishy frying pan. Add the wine and let it bubble fiercely, scraping up and stirring any sediment. Add the stock and continue boiling until well reduced (to about 6 tablespoons), by which time it will be syrupy.

3   Stir in the cream (and also the parsley if using it). Reheat. Check the seasoning and serve in a sauce-boat.

Serving suggestion: Grated courgette, salted, drained, left to degorge for 20 minutes, and then sautéd in butter with a pinch of thyme, makes a beautiful, light and unusual vegetable accompaniment to this dish. Allow one courgette per person.

Pan-Fried Salmon in White Wine

Serves 4

The wine in which the salmon is cooked will permeate the flesh of the fish deliciously. The seasoned flour acts as the thickener.

4 salmon steaks (170g/6oz each)
4 tablespoons seasoned flour
30g/1oz butter
1 wine glass white wine
salt and pepper

---

1   Turn the steaks quickly in the seasoned flour.

---

2   Melt the butter in a wide frying pan. When it is foaming, add the salmon steaks. Turn them over as soon as they have lightly browned.

---

3   Pour in the wine, bring to the boil, and then reduce the heat to a simmer. Cook for about 10 minutes. Spoon the wine over the steaks often during the cooking.

Serving suggestion: Try serving with a spring-like mixture of vegetables, such as baby corn, baby carrots, mange-tout peas, baby new potatoes and julienned courgette.

Salmon Steaks in Cream

Serves 4

This is a wonderful recipe. The cream seals in the juices, leaving the salmon tender and succulent. It is smart enough to serve at a dinner party and yet requires very little work, comes with its own sauce and is easy to serve.

4 salmon steaks, 170g/6oz each
250ml/10fl oz double or sour cream
squeeze of lemon juice
1 tablespoon chopped dill or parsley

1–2 tablespoons mild mustard
(Dijon)
seasoning
finely chopped parsley to garnish

Pre-heat oven to 180°C/350°F/Gas Mark 4.

1   Season the salmon steaks and sprinkle with lemon juice. (It is best not to do this too far in advance as the salt will draw the juices.)

2   Mix the cream with the dill or parsley, mustard and a few grindings of black pepper.

3   Place the steaks in an ovenproof dish in which they neatly fit, and spoon the cream mixture over them.

4   Bake for about 30 minutes, depending on the depth of the individual steaks, or until the top is lightly golden and bubbling.

6   Sprinkle with parsley.

Serving suggestion: This rather rich dish is well complemented with a few potatoes and a cool side-salad of watercress in a mustard vinaigrette.

Salmon and Sorrel Steaks

Serves 4

Sorrel is easy to grow and a delight to eat. As well as making a delicious accompaniment to fish, it adds its own style to herb flavoured sauces and butters and makes an unusual filling for omelettes. If you don't have sorrel, use spinach and add lemon juice.

4 salmon steaks (170g/6oz each)
450g/1lb sorrel
55g/2oz butter
salt and pepper
seasoned flour

For the sauce:
290ml/10fl oz fish stock
290ml/10fl oz white wine
110ml/4fl oz double cream

1   Put the fish stock and wine together in a pan and bring to the boil; reduce by half (to about 290ml/10fl oz).

2   Wash the sorrel; remove any large stalks. Place in a pan with half the butter and cook over a medium heat for 3 or 4 minutes. Season well.

3   Meanwhile, make the sauce: add the cream to the stock and reduce again until it is creamily thick.

4   Heat the remaining butter in a frying pan; dip the salmon in the seasoned flour and fry gently for 4 to 5 minutes on each side.

5   Arrange the salmon steaks on 4 plates. Reheat the sorrel briefly, and then spoon it into the steak cavities; to finish, pour the sauce over and around.

Serving suggestion: Thinly sliced potatoes, laid out slightly overlapping on a baking tray, brushed with oil and baked in a very hot oven for 10 minutes, are a crisp and flavoursome accompaniment to recipes like this.

Salmon Cutlets Augustus

Serves 4

For this, you could use fillets instead of cutlets of salmon, in which case spread the stuffing on top and reduce the cooking time to 20 minutes, basting with the butter and lemon (which make the sauce) after 15 minutes.

4 salmon cutlets (170g/6oz each)	*2 eggs*
1 small plaice, filleted	*2 tablespoons breadcrumbs*
110g/4oz button mushrooms	*45g/1 ½ oz butter, melted*
¼ teaspoon ground cloves	*60ml/2fl oz white wine*
pinch of ground nutmeg	*juice of 1 lemon*

Pre-heat oven to 190°C/375°F/Gas Mark 5.

---

1   Trim any fat, cartilage and bone from the cutlets, then scrape any flesh from the trimmings.

---

2   Put the good scraps in a food-processor with the plaice, mushrooms, nutmeg, cloves and seasoning. Add to this the breadcrumbs and eggs and mix well.

---

3   Lay the cutlets in a buttered ovenproof dish and spoon the fish forcemeat into the cavity of each piece of fish, curling the flaps around it to prevent drying out and for a neater appearance.

---

4   Baste with half of the melted butter. Pour the wine around them and sprinkle a few breadcrumbs over the top. Bake for 30 minutes.

---

5   Baste with the remaining butter, to which the lemon juice has been added. Return to the oven for a further 5 minutes before serving.

Serving suggestion: A small dish of steamed broccoli is ideal with this: the glowing emerald green sets it off beautifully.

Salmon Cooked in Champagne

Serves 5

This extravagant recipe can of course have white wine, preferably Chardonnay, substituted for the champagne. A traditional way to deal with salmon, it really does bring out its best qualities.

1.12kg/2lb 8oz middle cut salmon
3 shallots, finely chopped
225g/8oz mushrooms, finely
*   chopped*
½ bottle champagne or white wine

squeeze of lemon juice
200ml/7fl oz double cream
30g/1oz butter, cut into 4 pieces
salt and pepper

Pre-heat oven to 230°C/450°F/Gas Mark 8.

1   Place the mushrooms and shallots in a roasting pan, with the champagne. Lay the salmon on top and season; bake, uncovered, for 20 minutes.

2   When it is just cooked, remove the fish from the pan, skin it, wrap it well in foil, and return to the switched-off oven.

3   Strain the vegetables, reserving the liquid. Boil the liquid to reduce by a quarter. Add the cream and boil again. Meanwhile, liquidize the mushrooms and shallots. When the sauce is the consistency of thin cream, add the puréed mixture.

4   Finally, stir in the butter, a small piece at a time. Spoon some of the sauce over the fish, and decant the rest into a sauce-boat for the table.

Serving suggestion: A side dish of asparagus will complement this delicious and extravagant recipe.

Salmon Alexander

Serves 5

This is adapted from a very old English recipe. Originally, fresh oysters were called for, which are expensive, difficult to find and disappointing, I think, in cooked fish dishes: so I have substituted smoked tinned oysters which give it a subtle smoky taste, as well as giving the cook an easier time!

1 salmon fillet (900g or 2lb)
1 egg, beaten
1 tin smoked oysters (usually about
   100g/3½oz)
½ cup breadcrumbs (or 1 slice of
   bread, processed)
1 handful finely chopped parsley
pepper and salt

grated nutmeg
ground mace
30g/1oz butter
290ml/10fl oz water, plus 2
   teaspoons of tarragon vinegar, or
   150ml/5fl oz each of white wine
   and water
85ml/3fl oz double cream

Pre-heat oven to 200°C/400°F/Gas Mark 6.

1   Skin the salmon. Turn it skin side uppermost and make shallow slashes in the flesh. Cut the oysters in half. Mix with the breadcrumbs, nutmeg, mace, pepper and salt, and three-quarters of the parsley.

2   Brush the slashed salmon with beaten egg; spread the oyster seasoning over this, rubbing well into the incisions. Fold fillet in half, long side to long side, and tie in several places. If your fillet includes the tail end, fold this in so that the roll is of an even thickness. Lay fillet in a buttered ovenproof dish. Pour the wine and water (or vinegar water) around it; dot the top with butter, and season with salt and pepper. Cover with a lid or foil and bake for 1 hour.

3   Carefully transfer fillet to a serving dish or, alternatively, carefully strain the cooking liquid from the dish. Boil the liquid down to a quarter of its volume. Pour in the cream and remaining parsley. Bring back to the boil for a minute or two longer and serve poured over the fish.

Serving suggestion: Petits pois à la Française – peas stewed in butter on a bed of lettuce – make a fine accompaniment.

Salmon with Paprika

Serves 4

The powerful scent of the paprika is greatly softened by the cooking: its flavour is an unusual partner to salmon and remarkably good. The sauce is an elegant velouté and acts as a creamy foil to this.

675g/1lb 8oz salmon fillet
4 heaped teaspoons paprika
30g/1oz butter
salt

For the sauce:
25g/scant oz butter
25g/scant oz flour
290ml/10fl oz fish stock
4 tablespoons white wine
juice of ½ lemon
1 teaspoon finely chopped parsley

1   Skin the salmon fillet and divide into 4 pieces. Season each portion with salt and the paprika.

2   Make the sauce: melt the 25g/scant oz of butter and stir in the flour. Cook gently for one minute; then remove from the heat. Add the fish stock, lemon and wine, whisking all the time. When the mixture is smooth, return to the stove and stir until bubbling and the sauce has thickened. Lower the heat and allow to simmer for several minutes.

3   Melt the 30g/1oz piece of butter in a heavy frying pan and cook the salmon for about 4 minutes on each side, over a low heat as the paprika will burn easily.

4   Stir the parsley into the sauce and serve poured over the salmon.

Serving suggestion: A salad of blanched French beans and shallots, with a good vinaigrette poured over it while the beans are still warm, would be good.

Plaited Salmon with Beurre Montée

Serves 4

This is a lovely idea, unusual yet simple. It is also a good way of making a little expensive fish go a long way.

340g/12oz piece salmon, skinned
   and filleted
1 sole, or 170g/6oz turbot or halibut,
   skinned and filleted
570ml/1 pint fish stock

For the sauce:
290ml/10fl oz stock, reduced from
   above
110g/4oz unsalted butter
1 teaspoon flour
56ml/2fl oz double cream
2 tablespoons finely chopped chervil
salt and pepper

Pre-heat oven to 150°C/300°F/Gas Mark 2.

1 Cut the salmon, across the width of the fillet, into 16 even-sized strips. Ideally, about 15 × 1.5cm (6 × ½in).

2 Skin and fillet the sole. Cut each fillet into two, on the diagonal, leaving you with diamond shapes of a similar size to the lengths of salmon. You should have 8 pieces.

3 Plait together the strips of salmon and sole into 8 bundles; lay them carefully in a roasting pan.

4 Bring the stock to the boil. Pour carefully around the plaits and put the whole thing in the oven. The fish should be cooked in 6 minutes.

5 Meanwhile, cube the butter and return to the fridge until needed.

6 Carefully remove the fish from the pan with a fish slice, place on a dish and return to the turned-off oven to keep warm.

7 Strain the stock into a saucepan and bring to a rapid boil. Let it reduce by

half (down to 290ml/ ½ pint).

8   Meanwhile, melt 15g/½oz of the butter and stir in the flour. Cook for 1 minute, pour in the reduced stock, and stir until the sauce has come to the boil; then reduce the heat and let it simmer for at least 1 minute.

9   Stir the remaining butter in, one cube at a time, waiting for each to melt and be incorporated before adding the next. Finally, stir in the cream and chervil; check the seasoning – it will probably want pepper and a squeeze of lemon but not salt.

10   Flood four dinner plates with the sauce and lay the fish on top.

Serving suggestion: This can be served alone to make a perfect starter.

Salmon with Roquefort Sauce

Serves 4

The bold flavours of celery and blue cheese work well with salmon, as long as their quantities are strictly curbed.

675g/1lb 8oz salmon, skinned and
* filleted*
110g/4oz flaky pastry, rolled and
* folded*
court bouillon or fish stock,
* sufficient to cover salmon*
a little beaten egg
poppy seeds

For the sauce:
1 tablespoon chopped celery leaves
15g/½ oz butter
15g/½ oz flour
½ small stick of celery
30g/1oz Roquefort
1 small glass of white wine
3 small glasses fish stock (from
* above)*
1 small glass double cream
salt
pepper, or cayenne pepper

Pre-heat oven to: 220°C/425°F/Gas Mark 7.

1   Roll the pastry out very thinly, and cut into 12 fish shapes. Glaze with the egg and sprinkle with the poppy seeds. Bake for 8 to 10 minutes. Remove to a rack to cool and then reduce the heat to 190°C/375°F/Gas Mark 5 for the salmon.

2   Cut the celery into needleshreds. Blanch in boiling water for 30 seconds, then drain and leave on one side.

3   Sweat the chopped celery leaves in the butter over a very low heat; add the flour and cook for 1 minute, stirring constantly.

4   In a separate pan, reduce the wine by two-thirds.

5   Cut the salmon into 4 equal pieces. Lay in a roasting tin, pour the stock over them and cover. Bake until just done (about 20 minutes). Turn the oven down to a low heat.

6   Drain the stock from the fish; measure out 3 glasses and add to the reduced

wine. Return the salmon, well covered, to the warm oven. Put the pastry in too, to reheat.

7 Reduce the wine and stock, again by two-thirds. Add the cream and reduce by half. Season with salt and pepper or cayenne pepper. Pour this mixture on to the celery-leaf roux; mix until smooth. Bring to a simmer, stirring all the time; cook for 1 minute.

8 Stir in the celery needleshreds and the crumbled Roquefort. Reheat gently if necessary.

9 Flood 4 plates with the sauce. Lay the salmon on top and place the pastry fishes by the side.

Serving suggestion: This can be served alone, or with a vegetable such as spinach that will not detract from the fine celery garnish.

Salmon in a Spicy Crust

Serves 4

The deep colour and intense flavour of the spice coat combine beautifully with the pink and succulent salmon.

4 pieces of skinned, filleted salmon (170g/6oz each)
1 tablespoon of flour
3 teaspoons paprika
2 teaspoons cumin seeds
1 teaspoon coriander seeds
1 teaspoon cardamon seeds

2 teaspoons black peppercorns
salt
1 egg
55g/2oz butter
150ml/5fl oz hollandaise sauce (see page 114)

1   Grind the pepper, cardamon, cumin, and coriander, either in a coffee- or spice-grinder, or with a pestle and mortar. Mix the spices with the paprika and flour. Season with salt.

2   Add a pinch of salt to the egg and beat really well to break down any thick strands of albumen.

3   Dip the salmon first in the egg and then in the spice mixture.

4   Melt the butter in a heavy frying pan and when bubbling, add the fish. Cook over a gentle heat (the spices will burn easily) for 4 minutes on each side.

Serving suggestion: Serve with a salad of 'just cooked' broccoli in a sesame seed and lemon vinaigrette.

CHAPTER 3

SALMON AND PASTRY

Salmon Quiche

Serves 5

To use salmon in a quiche may sound strange, or even extravagant, but it is excellent. The two cheeses enrich and enhance it.

340g/12oz salmon, cooked and flaked
225g/8oz shortcrust pastry
30g/1oz grated Parmesan cheese and
* 30g/1oz grated Gruyère cheese, or*
* 55g/2oz Cheddar cheese*

1 tablespoon chopped chives, dill or
* parsley*
3 large eggs
150ml/5fl oz milk
150ml/5fl oz cream
salt, pepper and cayenne

Pre-heat oven to 220°C/425°F/Gas Mark 7.

1   Roll out the pastry, and line a 25cm (9–10in) quiche dish, or flan ring on a baking tray. Relax the pastry for 20 minutes, and then bake blind for 20 minutes. Allow to cool. Reduce the oven heat to 200°C/400°F/Gas Mark 6.

2   Beat the eggs, cream and milk, cheese(s) and a liberal amount of seasoning together. Place the salmon in the cool flan case, sprinkle with herbs and carefully pour the custard mixture over.

3   Return to the oven for 30–40 minutes at the lower temperature until golden and risen. Serve warm.

Serving suggestion: Green and peppery cress, if you grow it, would be perfect for this.

Salmon en Croûte

Serves 8

Crisp and light pastry complements the tender, moist flesh of salmon to perfection. It is a good way to cook fish because the flavour is sealed in.

1 whole salmon, skinned and　　　　　*dill, finely chopped*
　filleted (2.3kg/5lb)　　　　　　　*lemon juice*
450g/1lb flaky pastry　　　　　　　*seasoning*
15g/½ oz semolina　　　　　　　　*beaten egg or milk to glaze*
butter

Pre-heat oven to 230°C/450°F/Gas Mark 8.

1　Roll out about 170g (6oz) of the pastry to the thickness of a penny. Let it
relax for 20 minutes.

2　Skin the salmon and cut into 2 fillets. Cut the pastry into a fish shape
roughly the size of your salmon fillets. Prick all over and bake for 10 to 15
minutes until brown and crisp. Cool.

3　Sprinkle the semolina on the baked pastry case. You won't notice it when
the dish is cooked, but it absorbs any juices given out by the salmon, keeping
the pastry crisp.

4　Place the first fillet on the pastry and on to it spread the dill, salt, pepper,
little pieces of butter, and a squeeze of lemon juice. Place the second fillet on
top, roll out the remaining uncooked pastry and cover the fish. Trim the pastry
blanket to within 3cm (1in) of the base all round. Tuck this edge under the base.

5　Next, decorate your pastry fish. This can be as basic as an eye and mouth
marked with a knife, or you could do scales and the fins as well.

6　Glaze with the beaten egg and bake for 15 minutes in the hot oven of before,
then reduce the heat to 150°C/300°F/Gas mark 8 for another 30 minutes to
cook the fish.

Serving suggestion: Serve hot with a white wine and cream reduction sauce with dill, a beurre blanc or a hollandaise, or warm with mayonnaise or the Aigrellette sauce. A selection of vegetables, such as broccoli, carrots and mange-tout is ideal; the pastry negates the need of potatoes.

Koulibiac

Serves 6–8

According to Jane Grigson, although Russians commonly use rice in Koulibiac, the traditional grain to use is Kasha (buckwheat that is first roasted and then boiled like rice).

675g/1lb 8oz filleted salmon
225g/8oz shallots or mild onions, finely chopped
110g/4oz butter (preferably unsalted)
450g/1lb flaky pastry
225g/8oz of mushrooms
lemon juice
2 tablespoons chopped parsley
2 tablespoons chopped dill
grated nutmeg
seasoning
3 hard-boiled eggs, sliced
170g/6oz rice
stock (if using a stock cube, make up at half strength)
egg to glaze
290ml/10fl oz soured cream

Pre-heat oven to 200°C/400°F/Gas Mark 6.

1   Reserve a handful of the chopped onion, and cook the rest slowly in 30g (1oz) of the butter until they have become a soft, pale golden mass. Add the sliced mushrooms and stew until they have given up their juices (about 5 minutes). Add lemon juice and seasoning. Set aside.

2   Cook the remaining onions in 55g (2oz) of butter. When they too have softened down, add the rice. Stir constantly until it is coated in butter. Pour in the stock, bring to a simmer and cook until tender (about 20 minutes). By then the stock should have been absorbed and the rice will be moist. You will therefore have to watch the last 10 minutes, and add more liquid if necessary. Remove from the heat, season with the nutmeg, parsley, dill, pepper and salt.

3   Take the skinned filleted salmon. Cut it into thin slices. Fry these in another 30g (1oz) of butter, just for a few moments until they stiffen. (If you want to cut down on butter you can poach the salmon, in a piece, in the stock before you cook the rice. It must be only just cooked. Break it into large flakes, or slice, then continue with the recipe.)

4   Roll out 170g (6oz) of the pastry to an oblong. Lay on a baking sheet. Pile

on half the rice mixture, leaving the edges free. Place the slices of fish on top, then the hard-boiled eggs, the mushroom mixture, and finally the remaining rice. Glaze the margin.

5 Roll out the remaining pastry, and place it on top of the rice; seal carefully. Decorate the pie with pastry scraps; cut a steam hole in the top, and glaze.

6 Bake for about 45 minutes. Serve with a jug of seasoned sour cream.

Serving suggestion: Koulibiac needs nothing more than a bitter-leaved salad, such as curly endive.

Mushroom and Salmon Pie

Serves 4 to 5

My mother invented this for dinner when my husband's parents went to stay with them for the first time. Unfortunately, my father-in-law hates mushrooms! Nevertheless it was enjoyed by all.

225g/8oz flaky or shortcrust pastry
450g/1lb salmon fillet
450g/1lb whole button mushrooms
55g/2oz butter
55g/2oz flour

200ml/7fl oz stock and 200ml/7fl oz
*   milk, or 400ml/14fl oz milk*
salt and pepper
grated nutmeg
finely chopped parsley or dill
egg to glaze

Pre-heat oven to 230°C/450°F/Gas Mark 8.

1   Roll out the pastry and allow to relax.

2   Skin the fish, and cut into 3cm (1in) cubes, or pieces of a similar weight.

3   Wipe the mushrooms with a clean damp cloth. Trim the stalks if necessary. Melt the butter, add the mushrooms and allow them to stew gently.

4   After the mushroom juices have evaporated off, add the flour, stirring all the time. Remove from the heat after about 30 seconds, add the milk and stock (or all milk) bit by bit, mixing all the time until you have a smooth sauce. Return the pan to the heat, bring slowly to a simmer, stirring all the time.

5   When the sauce is gently bubbling and has thickened nicely (it should be thick enough to 'hold' the mushrooms), pour into a pie dish. Don't worry if it looks too thick: the salmon will release juices that thin it down. Season liberally with salt, pepper and nutmeg. Stir in the herbs. Allow to cool completely.

6   When the sauce is cold, add the cubed salmon. Cover with the pastry, crimping the edge against the pie dish. Decorate and glaze. Bake for 15 minutes, then lower the heat to 190°C/375°F/Gas mark 5 for another 15 minutes.

Serving suggestion: The pastry removes the need for potatoes. Serve instead baby corn mixed with broccoli for a beautifully colourful accompaniment.

Soured Cream Salmon Pie

Serves 8

This is a mixture similar to one you would use for a fish pie, but enriched with soured cream and cheese.

900g/2lb piece salmon
450g/1lb shortcrust or flaky pastry
55g/2oz butter
55g/2oz flour
pinch of cayenne pepper
pinch of dry mustard powder

500ml/1 pint stock or court bouillon
150ml/5fl oz sour cream
4 hard-boiled eggs, roughly chopped
170g/6oz strong Cheddar, grated
1 handful chopped parsley
1 egg to glaze

Pre-heat oven to 220°C/425°F/Gas Mark 7.

1   Roll out one-third of the pastry. Move to a baking sheet and allow to relax for at least 20 minutes. Prick all over and bake for 8 to 10 minutes. Roll out the remaining pastry and leave this to rest also.

2   Poach the salmon in the stock, in a piece, for about 20 minutes. Remove from the stock, skin it and break into large flakes while the fish liquor continues to reduce by half.

3   Melt the butter; stir in the flour, cayenne and mustard powder. Cook slowly for 1 minute, then add the reduced stock, whisking as you pour. Bring to the boil, and stir until very thick and smooth. Stir in the Cheddar, then the cream and parsley. Check the seasoning carefully.

4   Trim the cooked pastry base to a neat rectangle. Fold the salmon and eggs into the sauce which should be quite thick. Spoon on to the cooked pastry base to within 3cm (1in) of the edge. Lay the raw pastry over the top. Trim to 3cm (1in) of the base. Carefully fold this excess underneath.

5   Use the trimmings to decorate the pie. Glaze with the beaten egg and bake for about 40 minutes, reducing the heat to 190°C/375°F/Gas mark 5 after 15 minutes.

Serving suggestion: Serve with spinach.

Smoked Salmon Pie

Serves 6

This pie is made from a wickedly delicious pastry with layers of garlicky sour cream, dill and cheese. It may sound very rich, but served in the right environment with plenty of salads at a summer lunch it need be the only dish involving any real work or money. Try it as part of a buffet, too.

225g/8oz smoked salmon off-cuts
450g/1lb flaky pastry
55g/2oz Cheddar or Gruyère cheese,
  grated
30g/1oz Parmesan cheese, grated
85g/3oz melted butter
55g/2oz fresh breadcrumbs

2 tablespoons chopped fresh dill
1 clove garlic
150ml/5fl oz soured cream
lemon juice
black pepper
egg to glaze

Pre-heat oven to 200°C/400°F/Gas Mark 6.

1   Divide the pastry into 2 pieces. Roll each into a rectangle, one slightly larger than the other. Prick all over and bake the smaller one for 10 minutes, until semi-cooked.

2   Now for the fun bit of layering up! Mix the cheeses, butter and breadcrumbs together and season with black pepper. Scatter half the mixture over the semi-cooked base.

3   Chop the smoked salmon into pieces and lay them over the breadcrumbs. Make sure there is nothing within 3cm (1in) of the edge. Sprinkle the dill on top.

4   Mix the garlic and soured cream together. Season with pepper. Pour over the salmon. Sprinkle with lemon juice and top with the remaining cheese and breadcrumb mixture.

5   Brush the edge lightly with beaten egg. Lay the other half of the pastry over the top. Press the edges firmly together, crimping the edges with your two index fingers. Use any pastry trimmings to decorate the pie and glaze with more egg.

6   Bake for approximately 20 to 30 minutes, until the pastry is crisp and golden.

Serving suggestion: Equally good served hot or cold, with a bowl of salad leaves, a cucumber salad with mint vinaigrette and some hot new potatoes. Perfect!

Salmon in Filo Pastry with Watercress Mousseline

Serves 8

This is another ideal dinner party dish. It can be prepared ahead of time, looks wonderful with the pale pink and green, and is unusual yet delicious.

900g/2lb piece salmon, skinned and filleted
110g/4oz (or 2 bunches) watercress, well trimmed and picked over
8 eggs
55ml/2fl oz single cream

salt and pepper
olive oil
1 packet filo pastry
1 tablespoon of cumin seeds
lemon juice

Pre-heat oven to 200°C/400°F/Gas Mark 6.

---

1 Wash and pick over the watercress. Blanch briefly in boiling water and refresh in a bowl of cold water.

---

2 Liquidize the watercress, eggs, cream and seasoning until smooth.

---

3 Place in a double boiler, or in a bowl over barely simmering water. Whisk constantly until it is the consistency of double cream. Allow 30 minutes for this process. At regular intervals check that the water is not getting too hot or you run the risk of the mousseline curdling.

---

4 When it is done, place mousseline in a basin of cold water and whisk intermittently until it is cold.

---

5 Take an ovenproof dish, 25 × 35cm (10 × 14in) and 4cm (1½in) deep. Brush out with oil. Line with one very large sheet of filo, which comes well over the edges of the dish.

---

6 Cut out 12 sheets of filo pastry to fit the bottom of the dish. Layer these up, brushing with oil between layers as you go. Sprinkle the top sheet with cumin seeds and spoon over half the watercress cream.

7 Lay the salmon over the whole thing; season with black pepper and lemon juice. Add the remainder of the watercress mixture and smooth over.

8 Arrange a further 4 sheets of filo pastry on top, brushing each with a little oil. Fold in the overlapping edges, brush the whole thing with oil, lay one last piece over the top, and brush with oil again. With a sharp knife, lightly score the whole surface into diamond shapes.

9 Bake for 35–40 minutes. Serve hot or cold.

Serving suggestion: Serve with halved trimmed bulbs of fennel, boiled until just tender and then buttered, sprinkled with Parmesan, and baked until golden on top. Otherwise, a bowl of crisp green mange-tout makes a good alternative.

Individual Salmon Filo Koulibiacs

Serves 4 as a main course; 8 as a starter

These crispy pastry triangles would also be perfect for a picnic or, if reduced in size, they would make pretty canapés.

225g/8oz salmon filleted
290ml/10fl oz stock
110g/4oz rice
1 large shallot or ¼ mild onion,
    finely chopped
small piece of butter
2 tablespoons fresh dill, chopped

2 tablespoons fresh chives, chopped
6 tablespoons soured cream
1 hard-boiled egg, chopped
filo pastry
55g/2oz melted butter, or oil
seasoning

Pre-heat oven to 190°C/375°F/Gas Mark 5.

1   Bring the stock to the boil. Slip the salmon fillet in, bring back to a gentle simmer and poach the fish for 5 minutes. (The stock should be just moving, not bubbling.) Remove the fish, skin and flake it; reserve the stock for the rice.

2   Add some water to the stock and bring back to the boil; if it is your own stock add salt, but not if it is a commercial cube. When boiling, cook the rice until tender (about 20 minutes).

3   Meanwhile, sweat the shallot or mild onion in a little butter. When it is cool, stir in the cream, seasoning, herbs, rice, egg, and then, finally, carefully mix in the fish. (If you don't intend to bake the koulibiacs immediately, make sure everything is stone cold before combining.)

4   Cut the filo pastry into 8 long, thin, rectangular sheets, ideally 25cm × 10cm (10in × 4in). Brush lightly with oil or melted butter. Cover all but one sheet with a damp tea-towel.

5   Place one-eighth of the mixture across the top right-hand corner, to make a triangular-shaped mound. Flip this corner of the pastry over so that the top edge now meets the left-hand side of the rectangular strips. Repeat this folding all the way down, so that you are left with a triangular-shaped parcel, securely

wrapped, like a samosa. Repeat with the rest of the mixture and the remaining sheets of pastry.

6   Brush the parcel tops with any remaining butter or oil. Bake for about 25 minutes.

Serving suggestion: Serve hot, warm or cold, with a bunch of watercress to garnish. Individual koulibiacs are ideal for picnics: take along Little Gem lettuces, cut into 4 wedges, and seasoned sour cream to use as a dip.

Medieval Salmon in a Crust

Serves 8

Sweet flavourings were often used in medieval times with fish. This is a version of salmon en croûte that includes stem ginger and currants. Prepare to be surprised if you are someone who doesn't like sweetness in your savoury dishes: the combination works remarkably well.

1 whole salmon (2.3kg/5lb)
450g/1lb shortcrust pastry
2 knobs stem ginger in syrup
1 tablespoon currants

85g/3oz butter
seasoning
egg to glaze

Pre-heat oven to 220°C/425°F/Gas Mark 7.

1   Fillet the salmon into 2 pieces, and skin it, or get your fishmonger to do it. Season the fillets.

2   Roll out the pastry and allow it to relax.

3   Cream the butter. Finely chop the ginger. Spread two-thirds of the butter on to the first fillet and sprinkle the currants and ginger over this. Sandwich together with the remaining fish. Use the rest of the butter to spread on the top.

4   Lay the salmon on the pastry. Gather the edges of the pastry up, make a neat seam and pinch together; trim off any excess. Turn the whole thing over on to a flat baking tray, or on to the back of a roasting tin, so that the edges are underneath. Decorate and glaze.

5   Bake for 15 minutes. Reduce the heat to 180°C/350°F/Gas mark 4 and continue to bake for another 30 minutes.

Serving suggestion: Try a buttered julienne of carrots, with plenty of chopped parsley, as an accompaniment to this.

Torte de Saumon

Serves 10

This filling pie is excellent served for a lunch with salads. The mushrooms and butter ensure it stays moist so no sauce is needed.

900g/2lb salmon, boned and skinned	*6 tablespoons double cream*
1lb/450g shortcrust pastry	*85g/3oz butter*
450g/1lb mushrooms, finely chopped	*1 tablespoon finely chopped*
salt and pepper	*tarragon*
grated nutmeg	*1 tablespoon finely chopped chervil*

Pre-heat the oven to 190°C/375°F/Gas Mark 5.

1   Divide the pastry in two. Roll out each to a large circle; line a 25cm (10in) quiche dish with one piece and leave both this and the second piece of pastry to relax.

2   Cut 340g (12oz) of the salmon into small pieces, and mix this with the mushrooms.

3   Season with the salt, pepper and nutmeg. Bind together with the cream. Spread this mixture on to the tart base.

4   Slice the remaining piece of salmon into small thin pieces. Lay these evenly over the top of the salmon and mushroom mixture. Dot with the butter and season well.

5   Brush the edge of the tart dish with water. Lay the second piece of pastry over the top to form a lid. Crimp the edges to seal.

6   Bake for 30 to 40 minutes.

Serving suggestion: Tzatziki (the Greek salad of cucumber dressed in mint, garlic and yoghurt) and a bowl of lettuce will set this off beautifully.

Salmon Feuillettes with Spinach

Serves 4

This recipe may look time-consuming but it is worth it. You could use bought pastry to save time and even a good-quality frozen leaf spinach. Instead of using all salmon, try combining it with other fish, for example prawns, scallops or sole.

340g/12oz skinned fillet of salmon
450g/1lb of flaky pastry
1 egg for glaze
450g/1lb fresh spinach
nut of butter
grated nutmeg
570ml/1 pint fish stock

For the sauce:
5 tablespoons reduced stock (from above)
110g/4oz unsalted butter, cut into 8 pieces and returned to the fridge
1 level tablespoon finely chopped shallot
1 tablespoon white-wine vinegar
lemon juice
pepper

Pre-heat oven to 230°C/450°F/Gas Mark 8.

---

1   Roll out the pastry, and cut 4, thick diamond shapes of 11cm × 9cm (3½ × 4½in). These are going to be your feuillettes. Mark an inner line 3cm (1in) from the edge of the feuillettes, take a knife and lightly carve a zig-zag pattern within that border. Tap the edges of the pastry with the back of a knife blade to encourage the flakes to separate and rise during the baking. Leave to relax for 20 minutes.

---

2   Glaze the top of the pastry, being careful not to glaze the edges, then bake the feuillettes for about 15 to 20 minutes, or until they are risen and a good golden brown. Remove the 'cap' from the centre, scrape out any uncooked pastry. They may need to return to the oven for a few minutes, to dry out.

---

3   Wash and destalk the spinach. Place in a pan with some salt. (There is no need to add water, the moisture clinging to the leaves from washing will be enough.) Cook the spinach gently for 4 to 5 minutes, by which time it will have sunk right down and look very dark. Drain, and refresh in cold water. Squeeze

---

out as much water as possible. Return to the pan and add the nutmeg, butter and seasoning.

4   Cut the skinned and filleted salmon into 3cm (1in) cubes. Bring the fish stock to scalding point and add the salmon. The stock should be brought back to a simmer and then pulled off the heat. Remove the fish after 3 minutes and keep warm.

5   Reduce the stock down to 5 tablespoons. Add the shallot and the vinegar and return to the heat until reduced down to only 2 tablespoons. Lower the heat drastically and start to add the chilled cubes of butter, one at a time, whisking continuously. When one has melted, immediately add another. Do not let the sauce come near to a simmer. Season with pepper and lemon juice.

6   Meanwhile, reheat the pastry cases in the oven and the spinach in the pan.

7   Divide the spinach between the cases, then the salmon and pour the sauce over. Replace the pastry lids at an angle.

Serving suggestion: Serve with plainly boiled new potatoes if it is a main course, or by itself as a starter or fish course.

CHAPTER 4

MIXES AND MOUSSES

Salmon Mayonnaise

Serves 2 as a main course; 4 as a starter

The most obvious thing to combine with salmon is a good mayonnaise: together they are absolutely delicious and always taste as though they were made for each other.

225g/8oz cooked salmon
1 small Cos lettuce or endive
*100ml/3 ½ fl oz mayonnaise (*see
  page 120)

For the decoration:
4 anchovy fillets
4 black-stoned olives
6 radishes, sliced
1 hard-boiled egg, cut into 8 thin
  wedges

1   Wash and tear the lettuce into long strips (if using endive, halve the longer leaves). Arrange on 4 salad plates, or round the edge of a salad bowl.

2   Pile the fish, broken into generous-sized pieces, in the centre. Thin the mayonnaise with a little water (if necessary) so that it is the consistency of thick yoghurt, and cover the fish with it.

3   Now decorate with sliced radish, the egg, the pieces of anchovy fillet and the olives.

Serving suggestion: Serve alone as a starter; as a main course it will need no more than a crisp baked potato.

Salmon Cutlets

Serves 4

In this recipe, 'cutlets' actually mean little cakes of a salmon-based mixture, originally garnished with a piece of raw macaroni and a paper ruff, to look like a little lamb cutlet! Hard to believe that such an idea was once fashionable.

450g/1lb salmon
fish stock, or wine and water, sufficient
    to cover fish
15g/½ oz butter
225g/8oz mushrooms, finely sliced
15g/½ oz flour
110ml/4fl oz milk
grated nutmeg
1 bay leaf

1 slice of onion
1 clove
2 egg-yolks
seasoned flour
1 beaten egg
breadcrumbs
pinch of salt
oil or clarified butter

1   Poach the fish in the stock, or wine and water, until barely done. Remove from the liquid and cut into small dice. Set the liquid back on the heat to reduce to about 100ml (4fl oz).

2   Cook the mushrooms in the butter until all their liquid evaporates off.

3   Infuse the milk with the bay leaf, the slice of onion, clove, and the grated nutmeg. Strain.

4   Make the milk up to 200ml (7fl oz) with the stock reduction. Add the flour to the mushrooms and cook for 1 minute. Remove from the heat, pour in the strained liquid, and whisk until the sauce is smooth. Return to the heat, stirring all the time until it has come to the boil. Reduce the heat and simmer for a few minutes.

5   Stir the salmon into the sauce. Check the seasoning, which should be quite bold. Stir in the egg-yolks and allow to get cold. If possible, chill the mixture to make handling in the next stage easier.

6   Divide the mixture into 8 little cakes. Dip into seasoned flour, beaten egg and then breadcrumbs, seasoned with salt. Shallow fry in clarified butter or oil for 4 minutes on each side. Serve with beurre montée.

Salmon Pojarski

Serves 4

My husband and I ate these for breakfast in Poland, just outside Zakopane, served with soured cream.

450g/1lb salmon	*breadcrumbs*
3 slices bread (approx 170g/6oz)	*55g/2oz clarified butter*
milk	*150ml/5fl oz soured cream*
seasoned flour	*chives*
1 egg, beaten	*seasoning*

1   Skin and bone the salmon. Pound to a purée in a food-processor. Soak the bread in a little milk until it is sodden. (If you are not using sliced bread, the soaked purée should weight about 285g/10oz.)

2   Add the bread to the fish and season generously. Pat into 8 round cakes.

3   Flour, egg and breadcrumb the cakes. Fry in clarified butter over a medium heat for 4 minutes on each side.

4   Mix the chives into the soured cream and serve beside the salmon cakes.

Serving suggestion: Serve as part of a brunch.

Salmon Mornay

Serves 4

This may sound plain, but it makes a soothing and simple supper dish and has the virtue that it can be fully prepared in advance.

450g/1lb salmon, poached and
  flaked

For the sauce:
30g/1oz butter
30g/1oz flour
salt and pepper
grated nutmeg
pinch of mustard powder
290ml/10fl oz milk, or 150ml/5fl oz
  each of milk and stock
45g/1½ oz Cheddar or Gruyère
  cheese, grated
15g/½ oz Parmesan cheese, grated

Pre-heat oven to 200°C/400°F/Gas Mark 6.

1   Ideally, use 4 half scallop shells for this, otherwise have ready 4 individual ovenproof dishes.

2   Melt the butter; stir in the flour and the mustard powder, cook for 1 minute. Remove from the heat and pour in the milk, whisking until smooth. Return to the heat stirring all the time, it will thicken and come to the boil. Lower the heat and simmer for several minutes. Season generously with salt, pepper and nutmeg. Stir in the grated cheeses.

3   Divide the sauce between the scallop shells. Top with the flaked fish and season. Bake for 10 minutes.

Serving suggestion: Serve with braised celery or a salad, and bread.

Salmon Roe with Eggs

Serves 4 for brunch; 8 as a starter

A spoon of salmon roe has the appearance of a little heap of glistening pink pearls. They have an incredible taste, intense but not overpowering. They look really pretty against the background of the green and yellow mix of the chives and scrambled eggs.

1 small pot salmon roe
8 eggs
55g/2oz butter
2 tablespoons chives

salt and pepper
2 tablespoons cream
buttered toast with the crusts cut off
   (1 slice per person)

1   Melt the butter in a saucepan. Break the eggs into a bowl, beat well and season liberally. Add the cream and pour into the pan.

2   Over a low heat, stir the eggs constantly. It will probably take 10 minutes to heat up and then 5 more to scramble them. The slower they cook the more even and creamy will be their end appearance.

3   Stir in the chives. Spread the eggs on to the toast. Spoon the salmon roe into the middle of each piece. They should be slightly heaped, but not so much that the top of the heap is too remote to be warmed by the eggs. Serve immediately.

Salmon Kedgeree

Serves 7 or 8

Although smoked haddock is a more usual fish to use in this classic dish, salmon is a great favourite too. Some prefer to moisten it simply with butter, or a mixture of butter and cream. I personally think cream is the easier and gives a finer flavour.

900g/2lb salmon
fish stock, or wine and water
6 peppercorns
1 bay leaf
1 slice onion
225g/8oz brown basmati rice

150ml/5fl oz single cream
1 large bunch chives, snipped
2 tablespoons chopped parsley
6 hard-boiled eggs, coarsely chopped
salt and pepper

Pre-heat oven to 190°C/375°F/Gas Mark 5.

---

1   Lay the salmon in a pan with the stock, or wine and water, the peppercorns, bay leaf and onion. Bring to the boil and simmer until just cooked. Flake the fish from the skin and put to one side.

---

2   Put a saucepan of salted water on to boil. Rinse the rice thoroughly through a sieve, turn into the boiling water and cook for 25 minutes until tender.

---

3   Meanwhile, mix the cream, parsley, chives, eggs and the fish pieces in a bowl. Add the hot cooked rice and mix thoroughly. Check carefully for seasoning (it will probably need plenty).

---

4   Put the bowl into a medium oven for 15 to 20 minutes to finish reheating. Some people prefer to heat in a pan over hot water. When stirring, be careful not to break it up too much.

Serving suggestion: Traditionally, kedgeree is served with small triangles of toast.

Salmon Pancakes

Serves 4

Salmon pancakes can be prepared well in advance and even frozen. Unless you are catering for very hungry people, the pancakes remove the need for potatoes.

340g/12oz salmon, cooked and
flaked
30g/1oz butter
30g/1oz flour
150ml/5fl oz fish stock, or court
bouillon
85ml/3fl oz whipping or double cream
salt and pepper
cayenne pepper
1 tablespoon sherry

1 heaped tablespoon grated
Parmesan cheese
1 tablespoon finely chopped parsley

For the pancake mixture:
110g/4oz plain flour
pinch of salt
1 egg, plus 1 egg-yolk
290ml/10fl oz milk
1 tablespoon oil

Pre-heat oven to 200°C/400°F/Gas Mark 6.

---

1   First make the pancake mixture. Put the flour, salt, eggs, egg-yolk, and oil in a food-processor. While processing, pour the milk through the spout. Whizz until smooth, then pour into a bowl and leave to rest for half an hour. Alternatively, sift the flour and salt into a bowl. Beat the eggs. Make a well in the centre of the flour; drop the beaten eggs and oil into it. With a wooden spoon stir the milk slowly into the middle, incorporating a little of the flour with each movement until all is mixed to a smooth batter.

---

2   Now make the sauce. Melt the butter in a small pan. Add the 30g (1oz) flour and allow to cook for a minute. Remove from the heat and pour in the stock and cream, whisking until smooth. Return to the heat, stir constantly until thick and boiling. Lower the heat and allow to simmer for a few minutes. Remove from the heat, and stir in the Parmesan, sherry and parsley; adjust the seasoning.

---

3   Prove a crêpe pan or frying pan by rubbing with salt and oil. Wipe out, then brush lightly with oil. When hot, pour in a little of the pancake mixture, swirl it around until evenly spread and set. Thirty seconds later, turn over with a palette knife, cook for another 20 seconds, then turn out. Repeat with all the mixture. Even allowing for a few mistakes you should have enough to make 12 15cm (6in) pancakes and it is possible to get 17 from this mixture.

---

4 Stir the flaked salmon carefully into the sauce. Spoon the mixture on to the side of the pancakes that was cooked after turning, so that the more even colouring is on the outside. Roll each pancake up.

5 Lay the rolled pancakes side by side in an ovenproof dish. Cover with buttered foil and bake for 30 minutes, uncovering the dish for the last 5 minutes.

Serving suggestion: If you wish to serve the pancakes with a vegetable, try to select one that will introduce a different texture. For example, courgette sticks, salted, drained for 20 minutes, dried, tossed in seasoned flour and fried in butter, are ideal.

Salmon Soufflé

Serves 6 as a starter

The secret to a delicious soufflé is to have a good, flavoursome base. If you are cooking the salmon especially for this dish, cube it and marinate it first in a little wine and herbs. Poach in the marinade until just cooked (about 5 minutes for a fillet).

225g/8oz salmon, poached and flaked
55g/2oz butter
55g/2oz flour
290ml/10fl oz milk
grated nutmeg
1 bay leaf
1 slice onion

6 peppercorns
1 clove
55g/2oz Gruyère or Cheddar cheese,
  grated
30g/1oz Parmesan cheese, grated
salt, pepper and cayenne
5 eggs

Pre-heat oven to 200°C/400°F/Gas Mark 6.

---

1   Heat the oven with a baking tray in it. This will help to cook the soufflé more evenly.

---

2   Fork the salmon down to a paste. Season well, moistening it a little with some of the cooking juices.

---

3   Put the milk in a pan and heat to infuse with the bay leaf, grated nutmeg, peppercorns, onion and clove.

---

4   Meanwhile make the pannade: melt the butter, stir in the flour and cook for a minute. Remove from the heat and strain the milk on to it, whisking until smooth. Return to the heat and bring to the boil, stirring constantly. Lower the heat and simmer for a minute. (This is not a roux sauce, so don't be alarmed by how thick it is.)

---

5   Add the cheeses, seasoning and salmon to the pannade. Separate the eggs and whisk the egg-whites until stiff. Beat 4 of the egg-yolks into the pannade (discard the fifth), then stir in a large spoonful of the egg-white to lighten the mixture a little. Finally, carefully fold in the remaining egg-white using a large metal spoon, turning it as little as possible.

---

6 Spoon the mixture into a large, well buttered soufflé dish. Place in the oven, on the baking tray, for 40 minutes. When the soufflé is done it should move a little, but not wobble alarmingly, when the dish is given a little shove. Serve immediately.

Serving suggestion: The inside of the soufflé should still be a bit wet, so it serves as its own creamy sauce.

Salmon Mousse I

Serves 4

I love salmon mousse, whether it is for a smart summer lunch, in individual ramekins with toast as a starter, as a delicious supper with a cucumber salad and good bread, or even as a wonderful filling for sandwiches!

225g/8oz salmon, poached and
  flaked
11g/⅓oz gelatine (1 sachet)
1 tablespoon lemon juice
1 heaped tablespoon grated
  Parmesan or Cheddar cheese

1 tablespoon brandy, sherry or
  vermouth
2 tablespoons mayonnaise
2 egg-whites
salt and cayenne pepper
3 tablespoons water

1   Put the water into a small pan; sprinkle the gelatine on top and leave to 'sponge'.

2   Put the salmon, lemon juice, cheeses and brandy in a food-processor; season generously and purée.

3   Heat the gelatine very gently. When completely melted, add to the salmon mixture, pouring from a height to aid cooling, and stirring all the time.

4   Stir in the mayonnaise. At this stage, the flavour should be good, but strong. Leave in a cool place until it is beginning to set; this could be any time between five minutes and an hour depending on the outside temperature, so keep a careful eye on it.

5   When you see the mixture thickening, whip the egg-whites to stiffish peaks and fold in very carefully. If the egg-whites are added too soon your mousse will separate, if they are added too late it will be difficult to combine the whites without knocking the air out.

6   Spoon into ramekins, or a soufflé dish. If using a soufflé dish, run a knife through the mixture several times to ensure there are no large air pockets. Chill in a refrigerator.

Serving suggestion: Either serve from the dish, or turn out and decorate with paper-thin slices of cucumber.

Salmon Mousse II

Serves 8

450g/1lb salmon, cooked and
  flaked
8 slices smoked salmon
55g/2oz very soft butter
110ml/4fl oz soured cream or double
  cream

1 tablespoon sherry, wine, Noilly
  Pratt, or Madeira
salt and cayenne pepper
lemon juice

1 Mash the salmon down to a paste with a fork.

2 Cream the butter until light and fluffy. Beat in the alcohol then mix into the salmon.

3 Fold the soured cream into the salmon mixture; check the seasoning and add a little lemon juice. (If using double cream, first whip to floppy peaks and then fold in before adding the seasoning.)

4 Lightly oil 8 little ramekins. Line with the smoked salmon, making sure it comes over the edges of the pots. Divide the salmon mixture between the ramekins, then fold the excess smoked salmon over the tops. Chill until set. Alternatively, spoon some mixture on to one end of a slice of smoked salmon. Fold over once, then cut the remainder of the slice off; turn the parcel 90 degrees and wrap the salmon parcel in the other direction so that the mixture is completely enclosed. Again, chill until set.

5 When you want to serve them, run a knife round the edge to loosen them from their ramekins; give a sharp shake and place on individual plates with some salad leaves.

Serving suggestion: Serve on a little bed of chicory leaves or shredded lettuce.

Potted Salmon

Serves 12

This is my ideal dinner party starter: it is simple to make, can be made well in advance, and the flavour is superb. Potted meat was originally a way of storing the little scraps from a carcass: they were cooked until tender, then pounded and put into pots and sealed with clarified butter; in this way they kept for weeks. However, potted salmon is really a salmon paste, and is a bit of a cheat as I wouldn't like to keep it for more than a few days.

900g/2lb salmon, cooked and flaked
225g/8oz best-quality unsalted
  butter, softened
salt and pepper
ground mace
juice of 1 lemon
340g/12oz clarified butter (see page
  113), if the paste is to be stored

1   Cream the butter until very soft and pale. Mash the fish with a fork and then beat into the butter. Season well with the salt, pepper, mace and lemon juice.

2   Divide the mixture into individual ramekins. Pour the clarified butter over, making sure that although it is liquid it is not hot.

Serving suggestion: Serve cold but not chilled, with lots of hot toast.

Terrine of Salmon and Haddock

Serves 8

This simple terrine is perfect for a summer supper or as part of a buffet. It is a good basic recipe, very pretty, and perfect for adaptation if you so wished. The quantities can be halved to fill a 500g (1lb) loaf tin to serve 4 if this is required.

900g/2lb salmon
1 bay leaf
salt and pepper
150ml/5fl oz sherry
110g/4oz butter

675g/1lb 8oz haddock, whiting or
bass
2 egg-yolks
½ cup breadcrumbs/1 slice bread,
processed

Pre-heat oven to 170°C/325°F/Gas Mark 3.

1   Cut and trim the salmon into 5cm (2in) cubes. Marinate in the sherry with the bay leaf, salt and pepper, for at least 1 hour. Turn occasionally.

2   Pound the white fish to a paste in a food-processor. Add breadcrumbs, egg-yolks, butter, salt and pepper. Moisten with a little of the sherry marinade.

3   Butter a 1kg (2lb) loaf tin. Lay one-third of the white fish on the bottom of the tin; then half the salmon on top. Continue with a layer of another third of the white fish purée, then the remaining salmon, and finish with the last of the white fish.

4   Cover carefully with foil and bake in a bain-marie (a roasting tin filled with 3cm/1in of boiling water) for 75 minutes, until a skewer will glide in and come out clean.

5   When cold, place a weight of about 900g (2lb) on the terrine and press overnight. Place a tray under the tin to prevent excess liquid spilling over. Turn out.

Serving suggestion: Serve very cold in slices, with wedges of lemon and a green salad. A salad of broad beans, with skins removed after cooking, and dressed in a thyme-flavoured vinaigrette is ideal.

Sole and Salmon Chaudfroid

Serves 5 as a main course; 8 as a starter

These delicate and very beautiful little parcels can be served as a starter, as part of a buffet, or as a cold main course. Once, I even served them hot: after poaching them, I kept them warm while I made a velouté sauce with the cooking liquid; I served them with the sauce poured over, and with a little sprig of dill on each to top.

170g/6oz salmon, skinned and filleted	*20g/¾oz butter*
55ml/2fl oz double cream	*20g/¾oz flour*
1 egg-white	*290ml/10fl oz milk*
4 sole, skinned and filleted (keep the skin and bones for stock)	*1 blade mace*
	1 bay leaf
570ml/1 pint fish stock, with no trace of fat on it	*1 slice onion*
	4 peppercorns
55g/2oz gelatine	*salt and white pepper*
	dill

Pre-heat oven to 170°C/325°F/Gas Mark 3.

---

1   In a food-processor, pound the salmon with half the cream. Season well. Whisk the egg-white until it is well broken down and beat slowly into the salmon with a fork.

---

2   Divide the salmon mixture between the 16 sole fillets, laying it on the skinned side of each. Roll the fillets up and lay in a roasting tin. Pour 225ml (8fl oz) of the stock over them, cover with foil and poach in the oven until just cooked (between 10 and 15 minutes). Strain the liquid into a bowl and save. Re-cover the fish and allow to cool.

---

3   Meanwhile, make the aspic. Place 3 tablespoons of the remaining fish stock in a saucepan. Sprinkle the gelatine on top and allow to soak in. After a few minutes, heat very gently. When completely melted and clear, stir into the remainder of the stock.

---

4   Put the mace, peppercorns, bay leaf and onion slices in the milk and allow to infuse for a few minutes. Strain and add the reserved cooking liquid from the fish. In another pan melt the butter, add the flour and cook for a minute,

stirring continuously. Remove from the heat, pour the milky liquid in, whisking until smooth. Return to the heat, stirring until thickened and boiling. Lower the heat and allow to simmer for a few minutes.

5   Stir the remaining cream, salt and pepper and 200ml (7fl oz) of the aspic into the sauce. Allow to get cold but not to set.

6   Place the cold fish parcels on to a rack, with a plate underneath it. Spoon the sauce over them allowing it to fall in a smooth unblemished curtain. Pour the sauce that falls through the rack and on to the plate, back into the bowl and use to touch up any missed patches. Lay a tiny sprig of dill on each and allow to set.

7   Now trickle the cold but still liquid aspic over each parcel. Repeat again when this has set, for a glossier appearance. Leave to set.

Serving suggestion: When served as a main course, a salad of baby spinach leaves makes a good accompaniment.

Salmon Soup

Serves 6 as a main course

This soup is in the style of an American chowder. Flavoured with ginger, chilli and the smoky scent of oysters, the corn and potato provide the sturdy base, and the salmon – added last – is a delicate and delightful contrast.

450g/1lb salmon fillet, skinned
1 tin smoked oysters
4 tomatoes
2 cobs of corn, or 1 pack of baby
* corn*
3cm (1in) root ginger
1 or 2 chillis, to taste

2 medium potatoes
450g/1lb courgettes
1 onion
30g/1oz butter
1.7litres/3 pints fish stock
salt and pepper

1 Nick the skin of the tomatoes and then plunge in boiling water for 10 seconds; refresh under the cold tap. Peel, deseed and cut each into 8 strips.

2 Strip the kernels of corn from the cobs, by standing them upright on a plate and running a sharp knife downwards while slowly turning the cob round. If using baby corn, slice into pieces.

3 Peel and grate the ginger. Deseed the chilli and chop very finely. Cut the potato and courgette into dice. Finely chop the onion.

4 Sweat the vegetables in the butter, shaking the covered pan frequently, for 5 minutes. Add the stock and simmer for 15 minutes.

5 Cut the skinned salmon fillet into 3cm (1in) cubes. Drain the oysters from their oil. Add both to the vegetables; bring back to a gentle simmer, then turn the heat off. Cover the pan and leave for 5 minutes.

6 Check the seasoning (it may not need any).

Serving suggestion: Serve with plenty of really good brown or rye bread and unsalted butter, preferably thickly spread!

Salmon Fishcakes

Serves 4

These are truly delicious, but if you serve them with a beurre blanc or hollandaise they are difficult to stop eating! They can also be made with tinned salmon, but do check that it is not actually more expensive than the fresh fish. They will keep well in a warm oven so they can be prepared well in advance.

900g/2lb salmon
fish stock or wine and water
450g/1lb mashed potato
salt and pepper
55g/2oz melted butter
2 tablespoons parsley

a little milk
3 eggs
seasoned flour
breadcrumbs
clarified butter for frying

1   Poach the salmon in the stock, or wine and water, until it is barely done.

2   Break the fish up and add to the mashed potato. Beat 2 of the eggs. Add the butter, parsley and eggs to the fish, with plenty of seasoning.

3   If the mixture still looks a little dry, add some milk, but do not let it get sloppy. Shape into 12 rounds.

4   Beat the remaining egg. Flour, egg and breadcrumb the fishcakes. Melt the butter and fry the cakes over a medium heat for 3 or 4 minutes on each side.

Serving suggestion: Serve with a salad of raddiccio and curly endive, or other bitter salad leaves.

Terrine of Three

Serves 8

Although this is quite a lot of work, it is well worth it for the immense satisfaction there is in turning out the finished article from the tin. Very good for impressing people at dinner parties!

*225g/8oz salmon, skinned and
  filleted*
1 large sole, skinned and filleted

For the base mousse:
*675g/1lb 8oz whiting, skinned and
  filleted*
2 egg-whites
425ml/15fl oz double cream
1 teaspoon salt
½ teaspoon white pepper

For the herb mousse:
4 shallots, finely chopped
225ml/8fl oz dry white wine
½ teaspoon salt
¼ teaspoon white pepper
*110g/4oz spinach, washed,
  drained and destalked*
1 bunch watercress, washed

For the sauce:
1 beef tomato, skinned and deseeded
1 tablespoon red-wine vinegar
1 egg-yolk
225ml/8fl oz olive oil
cayenne pepper
1 teaspoon salt
¼ teaspoon pepper

Pre-heat oven to 180°C/350°F/Gas Mark 4.

1   First make the base mousse. Pound the whiting in a food-processor. Add half the double cream, the egg-whites, the 1 teaspoon of salt and the ½ teaspoon of pepper. Whisk the remaining cream and fold in.

2   Now make the herb mousse. Rapidly boil the finely chopped shallots in the wine, with the ½ teaspoon of salt and the ¼ teaspoon pepper. When the wine has reduced to 3 tablespoons, add the spinach and 30 seconds later the watercress. Boil until only 1 tablespoon of liquid remains. Process to a smooth paste, then fold in 3 tablespoons of the whiting mousse.

3   Grease a 1kg (2lb) loaf-tin. Line the bottom with grease-proof paper. Spread the base and sides with the whiting mousse, to a thickness of 1.5cm (½in).

4   Slice the salmon fillet horizontally into 1.5cm (½in) slices. Pound the sole fillets gently with a rolling pin to 7mm (¼in) thickness.

5   Place a layer of salmon fillet in the bottom of the tin, over the whiting base; top with another spread of whiting. Lay 2 of the sole fillets over this and cover with the herb mousse.

6   Now repeat the whole process in reverse, by covering the herb mousse with the remaining sole, more whiting mousse, the salmon fillets and then the rest of the whiting.

7   Cover with grease-proof paper, twisting under the rim of the tin to secure it and then repeat with a second layer of paper, this one dampened down with water first.

8   Bake in a bain-marie for 90 minutes. Weight lightly to encourage setting, and leave to cool.

9   For the sauce, liquidize the skinned, deseeded tomato with the salt, pepper, cayenne, the vinegar and egg-yolk. Add the oil, drop by drop, while the machine is running – as you would for mayonnaise.

10   When cold, turn the terrine out: dip the tin very briefly in a bowl of hot water, and then use a knife to ease the sides away from the mould to allow some air around it. (In order to achieve this, you may need to dip the mould again, but this is preferable to giving it too long in the hot water the first time, which will result in a half-melted, messy terrine.) Place a flat plate over the tin, turn the whole upside-down, and give it a sharp shake. You will hear a 'glug' and feel a transference of weight. (If you do not, turn the terrine back up and ease the knife round again before repeating the attempt.) Slice into 8 portions and transfer to plates with a little of the sauce on each.

Serving suggestion: If preferred, use Grellette sauce (*see* page 122) in place of the tomato-based sauce described here.

Salmon Terrine with Vegetables

Serves 6 as a starter

The vegetables chosen can be exchanged for anything you would prefer; for example try strips of grilled, skinned pepper, or carrot julienne cooked until tender.

450g/1lb salmon fillet, skinned
290ml/10fl oz fish stock
½ glass white wine
11g/⅓oz gelatine (1 sachet)
salt and pepper

170g/6oz broccoli
225g/8oz spinach
3 tomatoes
1 courgette

1   Divide the salmon into its 2 natural sections. Slice each section in 2 horizontally. Combine the stock and wine, and bring to the boil. Slide the salmon in, remove from the heat immediately and leave for 12 minutes until just cooked. Remove salmon.

2   Cut nearly all the stalk from the broccoli and blanch the little florets in the salmon cooking liquid for 3 to 4 minutes. Remember, a knife has to be able to glide through when cutting the terrine into slices, so they should be soft. Remove and refresh in cold water. Season lightly with salt and pepper.

3   Wash and remove any large stalks from the spinach. Place in a pan with just the water that clings to the leaves after washing, and a sprinkle of salt. Cook for a couple of minutes, during which time it will greatly reduce in bulk. Refresh in cold water, drain and squeeze thoroughly to remove all water. Chop finely and season.

4   Skin the tomatoes by making a small slash in their skins and then plunging them in boiling water for 10 seconds. Cut into quarters, remove the core and seeds.

5   Cut the courgette into neat julienne pieces. Blanch very briefly (about 30 seconds) in salty boiling water. Season.

6   Layer the prepared salmon and vegetables in a 500g (1lb) loaf tin or terrine mould in any way you wish, but the darker items, or deepest layers, look better at the very top or bottom. Julienned vegetables, such as the courgettes,

should be laid the length of the terrine.

7   Strain the stock through muslin. Remove a few spoonfuls to a small pan. Sprinkle on the gelatine and allow to sponge for a few minutes. Heat gently until clear and runny. Mix with the remaining stock and check it for seasoning. Cool until it is beginning to jelly, then pour slowly on to the terrine. Allow to set well.

8   To turn out: dip the tin or mould very briefly in a bowl of hot water. Use a knife to ease the sides away from the mould to allow some air around it. (In order to achieve this, it may be necessary to dip the mould again, but this is preferable to dipping for too long in the first place, which will result in a half-melted, messy terrine.) Place a flat plate over the tin, turn the whole upside-down, and give it a sharp shake. You will hear a 'glug' and feel a transference of weight. (If you do not, ease the knife round again before repeating the attempt.)

Serving suggestion: Serve on plain plates to set off the beautiful variety of colour and texture. Accompany with slices of walnut bread, toasted.

CHAPTER 5

SMOKED AND CURED

Smoked Salmon and Scrambled Eggs

Serves 4

Delicious for brunch or as a dinner party starter, this recipe is excellent for emergencies, as the ingredients are all to hand. There is no need to feel nervous about producing perfect scrambled eggs; the secret is patience. Allow up to 15 minutes when making scrambled eggs for four.

170g/6oz smoked salmon
8 eggs
55g/2oz butter

salt and pepper
1 bunch chives
4 slices buttered toast

---

1   Slice the smoked salmon into 3cm (1in) needleshreds. Chop the chives.

---

2   Melt the butter in a heavy-based saucepan. Whisk the eggs together with a fork. Season liberally with black pepper and very lightly with salt. Pour into the pan and set over a low heat. Meanwhile, warm the plates.

---

3   Stir the eggs constantly with a wooden spoon. It will seem that nothing is happening for the first 5 minutes, as the egg mixture slowly heats up. If egg flakes form too fast, take off the heat and continue stirring until the heat in the pan has reduced.

---

4   Continuing carefully like this will give you eggs with small even pieces. When they are thick but still too wet for your taste, add the salmon and chives. Stir for another 30 seconds or so, turn on to the toast and serve immediately.

Serving suggestion: If serving as a light lunch or supper, simply follow with a good green salad.

Lulu's Salmon Parcels

Serves 4

I have made these quite spicy, with Mexico's guacamole in mind. For a simpler tasting starter, you could leave out the tabasco and coriander.

225g/8oz smoked salmon	*salt and pepper*
½ ripe avocado	*pinch of sugar*
55g/2oz cream cheese	*juice of half a lemon*
1 clove garlic, crushed	*1 shallot, finely chopped*
½ tablespoon finely chopped	*2 tomatoes, skinned, deseeded and*
coriander	*chopped*
tabasco to taste	*dressed salad leaves to garnish*

1   Place the avocado, cream cheese, garlic, coriander, tabasco and seasonings (sugar, tabasco, lemon juice, salt and pepper) in the bowl of a food-processor. Whizz until smooth. Remove to a bowl and stir in the shallot and tomatoes. Adjust the seasoning.

2   Line 4 lightly oiled ramekin dishes with the smoked salmon, allowing the ends to hang over the pots' edges.

3   Spoon the mixture into the ramekins. Fold the excess salmon neatly over. Chill before serving.

4   To serve: run a knife around the edge of each pot. Invert on to your hand and give a sharp shake. When you feel the salmon drop down, slide on to individual plates.

Serving suggestion: Garnish with a few salad leaves torn small and dressed. Alternatively, use a few slices of avocado or more coriander.

Tabouleh Parcels

Serves 6 as a small starter

The nutty texture of the tabouleh combines well with the lightness of the lemony cucumber and the creaminess of the avocado.

450g/1lb good smoked salmon
½ ripe avocado
lemon juice
1 level dessertspoon finely chopped dill

10cm/3in cucumber
45g/1½oz cracked wheat
olive oil
salt and black pepper

1   Soak the wheat in a bowl of cold water, until it is tender when bitten into (about 1 hour). Drain in a sieve and turn into a clean tea-towel. Squeeze to remove as much water as possible.

2   Peel the cucumber. Cut into tiny dice about the size of large grains of rice. Place in a sieve and sprinkle with salt. Leave to drain for about 20 minutes. Place in a clean tea-towel and squeeze carefully to remove most of the salty cucumber juice.

3   Peel the avocado and cut into similar-sized pieces to the cucumber. Turn over in some lemon juice to prevent it oxidising.

4   Mix the wheat, cucumber and avocado together. Moisten with olive oil and more lemon juice if needed. Grind over plenty of black pepper, add some salt and the dill.

5   Lay the smoked salmon out, divided into 6 pieces. Place a spoon of the mixture in each and neatly roll up.

Serving suggestion: Serve with a wedge of lemon as a starter; the filling for these parcels can also be served as a salad.

Paupiettes of Salmon with Prawns

Serves 4

If tiger prawns are unavailable, it is really worth investing in top-quality prawns. Try to use the large, unshelled ones from the cold fishing grounds of the North for the best flavour.

450g/1lb smoked salmon
14 or 450g/1lb tiger prawns, or 30
    large, ordinary prawns
4 tablespoons fromage frais
1 dessertspoon grainy mustard

½ bunch watercress
1 bunch chives
1 tablespoon finely chopped chervil
1 tablespoon finely chopped parsley

1   Simmer the tiger prawns in salted water for 3 minutes. Cool and peel them. If using ready-cooked prawns, simply peel.

2   Blanch the watercress for 30 seconds, drain and refresh in a bowl of cold water. Squeeze all the water out and chop finely.

3   Stir the herbs, mustard and watercress purée into the fromage frais.

4   Lay the smoked salmon out on a board. Place the prawns down the centre of each slice. (If using tiger prawns, cut them in half first so that they lie in a straighter line.) Roll up from short side to short side. Work out how long the sausages are and cut the lengths into 20 even-sized pieces. Lay the paupiettes out in star shapes on the plates, 5 for each person. Spoon a little herb sauce into the centre of each plate.

Serving suggestion: Serve as a starter with lemon wedges.

Smoked Salmon Potato Gnocchi

Serves 4 as a starter

There are potato-cake recipes originating from many different countries. Most use 450g/1lb of potato to 110g/4oz of flour and 55g/2oz of butter. Fry potato cakes in butter for a delicious breakfast or supper. The Italians replace butter with egg and treat them like their gnocchi, which was what gave me the idea for this recipe.

55g/2oz smoked salmon
450g/1lb potatoes
110g/4oz plain flour
½ level teaspoon baking powder

1 egg
55g/2oz melted butter
30g/1oz Parmesan cheese, grated
salt and pepper

1   Peel and cook the potatoes until tender. Do not allow them to overcook or the paste will be too wet. Mash until smooth or sieve them – sieving gives a lighter finished dish.

2   Mix in the flour, baking powder, plenty of seasoning, and the egg. Spread out on a board, preferably a marble slab. Allow to get cold and set.

3   Cut the salmon into 28 pieces. Slice the potato mixture into the same number of cubes. Press a piece of salmon into each gnocchi cube, moulding the potato round to cover completely.

4   Put a large pan of water on to heat. When it is bubbling drop about half of the gnocchi in. Within 3 minutes they will bob to the surface. As they do so, remove with a slotted spoon to a heated buttered dish and keep warm. Add more gnocchi to the pan, continuing to remove when they come to the surface.

5   Keep the cooked smoked-salmon gnocchi warm. Between each layer add some of the butter and Parmesan. When all are done, drizzle over the rest of the butter and Parmesan and serve.

Serving suggestion: I would also serve this for a brunch, lunch or supper dish.

Smoked Salmon and Herb Salad

Serves 4

A lovely starter for the long warm evenings of summer. The aromatic oils from the herbs are a worthy partner for the smokiness of the salmon.

110g/4oz good smoked salmon, the
  best you can afford
1 bunch asparagus
6 leaves basil, washed and torn
6 leaves basil, finely chopped
2 tablespoons parsley, finely chopped
1 frond dill, washed and snipped
  with scissors
1 frond dill, finely chopped

2 eggs
1 bag mixed lettuces (about
  100g/4oz), washed and torn
1 small nut of butter

For the vinaigrette:
4 tablespoons olive oil
1 tablespoon lemon juice
salt and pepper

1   Beat the eggs in a bowl. Season well, adding the parsley, and the chopped dill and basil.

2   Melt the butter in a frying pan until it is frothy. Pour in half the egg mixture and swill about until it covers the whole pan thinly. Cook gently, then turn out on to a plate. Repeat with the remaining egg mixture. Place the second thin omelette on top of the first and roll them up together. Slice the roll up, making long noodle-like strips of cooked egg.

3   Turn the lettuce, whole basil leaves and snipped dill into a bowl.

4   Brutally trim down the asparagus, leaving you with spears of about 8cm (3in). (Keep the trimmings to make soup.) Steam or boil the tips for 4 to 6 minutes, depending on their thickness and freshness. Plunge into a bowl of cold water the minute they are tender, and then drain.

5   Mix the oil, lemon, pepper and salt, to make the vinaigrette.

6   Add the asparagus to the lettuce and herbs; then add the eggs. Slice the smoked salmon into pieces similar to the egg strips and add to the salad. Before serving, dress with the lemon vinaigrette.

Serving suggestion: Serve with good bread for a light lunch, or alone as a starter.

Three Way Salmon

Serves 4

This is a good dinner party starter. It is not too much work, and yet it is quite unusual. The two sauces are mayonnaise and crème fraîche based.

1 slice smoked salmon, cut into 4
  (approx. 85g/3oz)
12 slices gravad lax (see page 94)
55g/2oz cooked salmon
110ml/4fl oz double cream, chilled
1 lemon
1 lime
salt and pepper

cayenne
4 dessertspoons mayonnaise (see
  page 120)
pinch of saffron
4 dessertspoons crème fraîche
6 slices wholemeal bread
1 handful torn mixed lettuces, or
  1 bunch watercress

1   Infuse the saffron in a drop of boiling water for 30 minutes. Slice half the lime and half the lemon into 4 thin slices each, for the garnish.

2   Pound the cooked salmon in a pestle or a food-processor. Add a squeeze of lemon juice, the cayenne, seasonings and the double cream in 5 or 6 even stages. Chill.

3   Add a squeeze of lime juice to the crème fraîche and season. Stir the saffron into the mayonnaise. Check the seasoning of both sauces.

4   Toast the bread and cut out 2 circles (each 5cm/2in diameter) from each slice.

5   Place 3 croûtes on each plate. On the middle croûte pipe some salmon pâté. On the other two, place 3 slices of gravad lax and one of smoked salmon. Place a spoonful of each sauce either side of each croûte. Garnish with the lettuce, lemon and lime.

Smoked Salmon and Ceviche Pâté

Serves 6

I use this recipe for individual pâtés a lot. They are easy to make, look absolutely stunning and are quite delicious. Perfect for a dinner party starter.

285g/10oz good smoked salmon
285g/10oz very fresh white fish
  (whiting or haddock)
juice of 1 lemon
olive oil
1 tablespoon finely chopped parsley

1 tablespoon finely chopped dill
salt and pepper
110g/4oz soft cream cheese
6 sprigs dill to garnish

1   Skin and bone the white fish. Roughly process or chop finely; add the lemon juice. Cover and leave in a cool place for about an hour until the fish has lost its translucent look. This is based on the South American way of serving fish, a method known as 'ceviche'.

2   Brush 6 ramekins lightly with oil. Place a small sprig of dill at the bottom of each dish.

3   Line the ramekins with the smoked salmon, allowing the ends to hang over the edges. Trim the excess and reserve.

4   When the white fish is sufficiently marinated, drain. Now process again with the cream cheese, a little olive oil, a little of the lemony fish juices, the finely chopped parsley and dill, and any left-over smoked salmon.

5   Taste. Adjust the balance of the flavours if necessary, remembering the saltiness of the smoked salmon.

6   Divide the fish mixture between the ramekins and smooth. Fold over the over-hanging ends of smoked salmon and chill for at least 4 hours. They turn out quite easily; simply run a knife round and invert on individual plates.

Serving suggestion: Decorate with salad leaves of differing colours and textures, and serve with oatcakes.

Marinated Salmon I

Serves 4 as a starter

This recipe must use only the freshest salmon, as it is virtually raw, having a very short marinading time.

225g/8oz salmon, skinned and
    filleted
2 large limes
4 tablespoons snipped chives
2 tablespoons finely chopped chervil

1 heaped tablespoon mild French
    mustard
1 dessertspoon olive oil
salt and pepper

---

1   Slice the salmon into the thinnest possible slices. Lay out on a large plate.

---

2   Squeeze the lime juice into a jar, snip the chives into it with the oil, chervil and mustard. Screw on the lid and shake until emulsified. Season to taste. Pour over the salmon and leave for 15 minutes.

D.H.T.

Marinated Salmon II and Melon Salad

Serves 5 as a starter

The sweetness of the melon marries well with the lime-impregnated richness of the salmon, and a little goes a long way.

340g/12oz very fresh salmon fillet,
  skinned
juice of 2 limes
1 heaped teaspoon green
  peppercorns (if tinned, rinse
  well first)
1 small ripe melon
salt and pepper

mixture of salad leaves (such as
  raddiccio, curly endive and
  lollo rosso), torn quite small
4 tablespoons olive oil
1 tablespoon vinegar
pinch of sugar
pinch of dry mustard

1   Slice the salmon as thinly as possible. Brush with the lime juice, then sprinkle with the green peppercorns. Refrigerate, covered, overnight or for a minimum of 12 hours.

2   Mix the oil, vinegar, and seasonings together. Turn the prepared salad leaves in the dressing and divide between 5 plates.

3   Slice the melon into 20 slices, with the skin cut off. Arrange the salmon interleaved with the melon slices on top of the salad.

Gravad Lax

A 2.3kg (5lb) salmon will feed 20 as a starter

Gravad lax is the now very popular Scandinavian alternative to smoked salmon. It is a 'pickled' fish. Recipes vary enormously in the timing and quantities of salt, sugar and pepper. Some add a little brandy, others lemon or vinegar. This version seems to hover nearest the middle, but they are all delicious. It is best to use a whole fish, as here, but 1kg (2lb) of boned middle cut will suffice.

1 whole salmon	*sugar*
sea salt	*brandy*
white peppercorns	*olive oil*
lots of dill	

1   Fillet the salmon into 2 large pieces, keeping the skin on. Do not rinse the fish. Smear both fillets with oil. Cut a generous amount of dill fronds on to the flesh of one fillet. Mix together equal quantities of sugar and salt. Pack on to the flesh – on top of the dill – to a depth of about 1.5cm (½in). If the fillets are thinner than usual use a little less.

2   Splash a little brandy over this and sprinkle heavily with crushed white peppercorns. Snip more dill over the pepper and sandwich with the second fillet.

3   Wrap well but loosely several times in foil. Place on a plate, with a board or tray on top of the salmon. Weigh down with several large cans. Leave at room temperature for 8 hours, turning the whole thing over and weighing down again after 4 hours. Refrigerate for a further 4 hours after this before serving.

4   If you would prefer, you can marinade the fish for 48 hours in a cool place with less weight on top (or even for 3 days, although in this case I would want to refrigerate it).

5   To serve, scrape off any excess dill coating. Place a fillet on a board and cut thin, vertical slices so that each piece has a pretty top line of dill and the skin is left behind.

Serving suggestion: Serve with dill and mustard sauce (*see* page 123), and brown bread and butter.

CHAPTER 6

CANAPÉS

Asparagus with Salmon Pâté

Makes 24 canapés

You could switch the salmon pâté for one made with smoked salmon; it must, however, be quite mild to ensure appreciation of the asparagus's flavour.

12 spears asparagus
5 slices bread
2 tablespoons mint jelly
1 scant tablespoon tarragon vinegar

For the pâté:
110g/4oz salmon, cooked and flaked
15g/½ oz grated Parmesan cheese
60ml/2fl oz soured cream
lemon juice
salt and pepper

1   Break up the salmon with a fork. Beat in the soured cream and Parmesan. Season with salt, pepper and lemon juice.

2   Cut the asparagus down leaving spears of about 5cm (2in). Blanch in boiling water until just tender (about 3 minutes). Cool quickly in a bowl of cold water.

3   Make toast from the sliced bread. Cut the crusts off, leaving rectangles, which should then each be cut into 5 slices of a similar size to the asparagus spears.

4   Gently heat the mint jelly and vinegar until melted. Pipe or spread a little salmon pâté on to each piece of toast. Slice the asparagus spears in half horizontally. Lay a half-spear on each canapé, flower side up.

5   Brush these lightly with the mint jelly and allow to set. If you want to make these canapés more than 1 hour in advance, fry the bread instead of toasting it.

Smoked Salmon with Basil and Mozzarella

Makes 24 canapés

The creamy blandness of mozzarella complements both the salmon and the flavour of basil.

225g/8oz smoked salmon
1 wet mozzarella (about 170g/6oz)
12 large basil leaves
olive oil
lemon juice
black pepper

---

1   Slice the mozzarella into 24 batons of about 1cm × 4cm (½ × 1½in). Chop the basil quite finely and sprinkle over the mozzarella. Add a squeeze of lemon, some black pepper and moisten with olive oil.

---

2   Leave overnight if possible. Cut the salmon into pieces large enough to wrap around each mozzarella stick. Roll them up individually and chill until ready to serve. Pierce each baton with a cocktail stick.

Spinach and Salmon Roulade

Makes 30 canapés; serves 4 as a starter

If using as a starter, do not split the spinach base into 2 parts; and slice the finished roulade into 8 or 12 rounds, rather than 30.

110g/4oz smoked salmon pieces
170g/6oz frozen leaf spinach
8g/¼ oz butter
salt and pepper

2 eggs, separated
nutmeg, grated
150ml/5fl oz soured cream
1 teaspoon finely chopped dill

Pre-heat oven to 200°C/400°F/Gas Mark 6.

1   Line a Swiss-roll tin (20 × 25cm/8 × 10in) with silicone paper.

2   Cook the spinach, drain thoroughly, and then purée. Beat in the piece of butter with some salt and pepper and the nutmeg. Stir in the egg-yolks; finally, whisk the egg-whites to stiff peaks and carefully fold into the mixture.

3   Pour into the Swiss-roll tin and smooth over; bake for 10 to 12 minutes, until firm to the touch.

4   Turn out on to a piece of grease-proof paper. Cut in half lengthways. Spread both pieces first with the sour cream to which the dill has been added and then the smoked salmon. Roll them both up individually, from long edge to long edge.

5   Dampen some grease-proof paper and wrap each roulade up in it. Put back in the oven for a further 5 minutes to set.

6   Allow to cool and then chill before slicing each roll into 15 slices.

Dill Pancakes with Two Fillings

Makes 24 of each type

Pancakes freeze very well, so they can be made well in advance.

For the pancakes:
110g/4oz plain flour
pinch of salt
1 egg
1 egg-yolk
150ml/5fl oz milk
150ml/5fl oz water
1 tablespoon oil
1 tablespoon finely chopped dill

Filling 1:
85g/3oz smoked salmon pâté
(see page 102)

Filling 2:
12 asparagus spears
a little mayonnaise
55g/2oz smoked salmon

1   Put the flour, pinch of salt, eggs and oil in a food-processor. Switch on and pour the milk and water through the spout. Pour into a bowl and allow to rest for 30 minutes. If preparing the batter by hand, sift the flour and salt into a bowl. Make a well in the centre and add the oil and beaten eggs. With a wooden spoon stir the eggs, slowly adding the milk and water, incorporating a little of the flour with each movement, until all is combined into a smooth batter. Leave to rest.

2   Meanwhile boil the asparagus tips until just done (2 to 4 minutes depending on thickness and freshness).

3   Prove the crêpe pan or frying pan by rubbing out with oil and salt. Wipe clean, then brush lightly with oil, and heat. When it begins to smoke pour a little mixture in, swirl it around until evenly and thinly spread. Allow to set. After 30 seconds, turn over with a palette knife, cook for another 20 seconds then remove. Repeat with all the mixture. You should have at least 12 15cm (6in) pancakes, even allowing for mistakes.

4   Stamp out 4 rounds from each pancake. Place a little teaspoon of smoked salmon pâté in 24 of the cut-outs. Curl one edge over to make a cone shape, allowing the pâté to show at the wide end. With the remaining pancake rounds, place a little piece of smoked salmon on each. Halve the asparagus spears vertically. Place a tiny blob of mayonnaise on each piece of salmon and top with a half asparagus spear. Roll the pancake so that the tip of the asparagus and a flash of pink show.

Smoked Trout and Salmon Parcels

Makes 16 canapés

The secret with these is to keep them small; otherwise they are too rich. If the weather is hot, whisking the cream first may help to keep the mixture firm. Otherwise you could replace cream with cream cheese.

85g/3oz smoked trout
170g/6oz smoked salmon
1 teaspoon grated horseradish, or
*   hot horseradish relish, or*
*   horseradish mustard*

black pepper
lemon juice
a little double cream
chervil to garnish

1   Remove the skin and bone from the trout. Whizz to a paste in a food-processor with the pepper, lemon and horseradish to taste. Moisten with cream but don't allow to get too soft. (The smoked salmon needs lemon, too, so bear this in mind when making the trout pâté.)

2   Cut the salmon into 24 strips 4cm (1½in) wide. Place a small teaspoon of the trout pâté on each strip. Roll over once and cut off the remainder of the strip. Turn the parcel around by 90 degrees. Roll over again so that the trout is completely hidden in a neat parcel. Decorate with a tiny sprig of chervil. Chill.

Salmon Strudels

Makes 32 canapés

The fillings for this are infinitely variable. You could make miniature koulibiac pastries; or exclude the mushrooms, adding chervil as a contrasting flavour instead.

110g/4oz salmon, poached and
  flaked
1 small nut of butter
1 shallot, finely minced
110g/4oz mushrooms, diced

1 tablespoon dill
melted butter
filo pastry
1 beaten egg

Pre-heat oven to 200°C/400°F/Gas Mark 6.

1   Sweat the shallot in the butter until soft and translucent. Add the mushrooms; cook until their juices are released and have evaporated off.

2   Mix the salmon and dill into the mushrooms. Season liberally.

3   Lay out a sheet of filo. Brush with melted butter. Cut it into long strips 4cm (1½in) wide.

4   Place a small teaspoon of mixture at the lower end of a filo strip. Fold the lower right-hand corner over the salmon to meet the opposite edge of the strip. Now fold the protruding corner over and upwards so that 2 sides are sealed. Next, fold over the lower left-hand corner leaving you with a neatly sealed triangular parcel. Repeat until the strip is no longer wide enough for the growing size of the strudel. Trim at this point.

5   Repeat the procedure with the other filo strips until all the mixture is used up. Brush the parcels with beaten egg and bake on a greased baking tray for 15 to 20 minutes. Serve hot.

Salmon Crackers

Makes 30 canapés

The secret with these pretty little filo shapes is to cook them in a very hot oven. For this reason, do not cook more than one batch at a time, so as not to lower the oven temperature more than is necessary. Always work quickly with filo pastry, keeping unused pastry well wrapped up at all times. (Left-over filo can be successfully frozen, as long as it was fresh, not frozen, when bought.)

170g/6oz salmon fillet, skinned
3 tablespoons lemon juice
1 teaspoon finely chopped dill
6 sheets filo pastry
melted butter
beaten egg

Pre-heat oven to 220°C/425°F/Gas Mark 7.

1   Place the salmon in a bowl with the lemon and marinate for at least 30 minutes. Cut into 5 × 1cm (2 × ½in) strips.

2   Lay out a sheet of filo pastry; brush with melted butter and top with another piece. Brush this with butter too. Cut the pastry into rectangles 5 × 10cm (2 × 4in). You should get 7 along the length of the sheet and 3 along the top.

3   Dry each piece of salmon on a clean tea-towel; place a salmon piece on the edge of a filo square and roll up. Pinch the ends together to make cracker shapes.

4   Brush with beaten egg and lay them out on a large baking sheet, with plenty of space between each. Bake for 10 minutes. Serve hot.

Choux Buns with Smoked Salmon Pâté

Makes 30 canapés

Choux pastry makes a good vehicle for canapés as they dry out in the oven, leaving small crisp empty shells.

For the choux buns:
30g/1oz butter
70ml/2½fl oz water
35g/1¼oz plain flour, sifted twice
1 large egg

For the smoked salmon pâté:
85g/3oz smoked salmon
140g/5oz cream cheese
salt and black pepper
lemon juice
paprika
dill

Pre-heat oven to 200°C/400°F/Gas Mark 6.

1   Sift the flour twice, on to a piece of paper. Place the butter and water in a pan and heat. When the butter has melted, bring to the boil. As soon as the water is boiling fast, remove from the heat, and tip the sifted flour in. Beat immediately with a wooden spoon until the mixture has formed a smooth paste.

2   Whisk the egg with a pinch of salt. When the flour mixture (choux paste) is cold, start to add the egg a little at a time beating well in between additions. The more you beat, the more egg the choux paste will take, giving better final results. The mixture should be smooth and shiny and drop off the spoon in one heavy blob. Don't make it soft by adding too much egg.

3   With two spoons, push half-teaspoons of the choux paste on to a non-stick baking sheet. Bake for about 10 to 15 minutes until dry, crisp and browned.

4   Chop the smoked salmon to a paste in a food-processor. Add the cream cheese, then the lemon, dill and paprika to taste. Fill a small nozzled piping bag with the mixture.

5   Slice each miniature profiterole across the top, almost in two; pipe a little mixture in and sandwich the lid back down.

Salmon Aigrettes

Makes 20 canapés

Aigrettes are deep-fried spoons of choux pastry. Usually they are simply cheese flavoured, but in this recipe I have added lemony salmon as a surprise filling.

*85g/3oz salmon, skinned and
  filleted*
juice of ½ lemon
½ clove garlic
paprika
oil for deep frying

For the choux paste:
30g/1oz butter
70ml/2½ fl oz water
35g/1¼ oz plain flour, sifted twice
55g/2oz Cheddar cheese, grated
1 large egg
pinch of salt

1   Cut the salmon into 20 even-sized pieces. Marinade in the lemon juice, garlic and paprika for 1 hour.

2   Meanwhile, make the choux paste: sift the flour twice, onto a piece of paper. Place the butter and water in a pan and heat. When the butter has melted, bring to the boil.

3   As soon as the water is boiling fast, remove from the heat, and tip the sifted flour in. Beat immediately with a wooden spoon until the mixture has formed a smooth paste. Stir in the grated cheese.

4   Whisk the egg with a pinch of salt. When the flour mixture (choux paste) is cold, start to add the egg a little at a time beating really well in between additions. The more you beat, the more egg the mixture will take, giving better end results. The mixture should be smooth and shiny and drop off the spoon in one heavy blob. Don't make it soft by adding too much egg.

5   Strain the marinade from the salmon. Take a teaspoon of the salmon in one hand; with the other, scoop a little choux paste on to another teaspoon and manoeuvre around the salmon until the fish is fully covered.

6   When all are done, deep fry until they turn brown and bob to the surface. Drain on absorbent paper and serve immediately.

Smoked Salmon Catherine Wheels

Makes 36 canapés

The beauty of these 'Catherine wheels' is not only that they look interesting, but that they use up any smoked salmon scraps. (Off-cuts should not be used because they are rarely of a good enough quality.)

170g/6oz smoked salmon
6 slices brown bread
a little water
softened butter
lemon juice
black pepper

1   Cut the crusts off the sliced bread and separate into pairs. Sprinkle each slice lightly with water. Lay one slice slightly over another, end to end; there should be an overlap of about 1cm (½in). Repeat with the other 2 pairs of slices.

2   Roll the bread flat, crushing the overlap down with a rolling pin. Repeat with the remaining pairs to make 3 large slices. Spread with the butter.

3   Lay the salmon out over these, leaving a 1cm (½in) gap on one of the long edges of each piece of bread. Score along this edge with a knife. Season the salmon with pepper and lemon juice.

4   Roll up lengthways, starting from the scored side; this gives a neat, tight centre to the roll. You will now have 3 long, thin Swiss rolls of salmon. Wrap in cling-film and chill.

5   Slice each roll into about 12 pieces, and arrange flat on a plate so that people can see the pink swirl.

Salmon with Brown Bread and Butter

Makes 16 or 20 canapés

This is the very simplest and probably the most delicious way to serve smoked salmon. Use really good bread and best unsalted butter to complement the tender smokiness of the salmon.

110g/4oz good smoked salmon, the best you can afford
4 or 5 slices from a loaf of very fresh granary bread
soft, unsalted, or slightly salted, butter
1 lemon
black pepper

---

1   Butter the bread, grind black pepper over each slice. Arrange the salmon neatly on it. Cut the crusts off and cut each slice into 4 triangular pieces.

---

2   Slice the ends off the lemon. Halve it lengthways and then cut each half into 3 wedges. Squeeze 1 wedge over the salmon.

---

3   Arrange the triangles on a plate with the remaining lemon wedges.

Gravad Lax on Pumpernickel

Makes 24 canapés

Pumpernickel has a splendid punchy 'sour' flavour that marries wonderfully with the richness of gravad lax.

6 slices pumpernickel bread
butter
1 tablespoon mild French mustard
a little icing sugar
1 box of cress
170g/6oz gravad lax

1   Butter the pumpernickel and cut each slice into 4 squares.

2   Sweeten the mustard with a little icing sugar, to suit your own taste. (Bear in mind the sourness of the pumpernickel and the flavour of gravad lax.) Spread thinly over the butter.

3   Cut the cress and lay a neat line over each piece of bread.

4   Finally, cover this with slices of gravad lax, allowing the leafy heads of the cress to show at one side.

Smoked Salmon on Rye Bread

Makes 30 canapés

The mustard and dill flavours of the sauce, traditionally served with gravad lax, are also interesting with smoked salmon in a small mouthful.

5 or 6 pieces rye bread, thinly sliced
3 dessertspoons mayonnaise
1 tablespoon French or Dijon
   mustard

1 tablespoon dill, finely chopped
55g/2oz smoked salmon
lollo rosso salad leaves
dill fronds to garnish

1   Mix the chopped dill and mustard into the mayonnaise.

2   Spread slices of rye bread thinly with this mixture, before stamping out 24 rounds, 3cm (1in) in diameter, avoiding the crusts.

3   Wash the lollo rosso really well and dry gently with a clean tea-towel. Tear off little pieces, ensuring each has a little of the frill. Place these on the rye-bread rounds.

4   Next add a tiny blob of the mayonnaise and top with 3 × 1cm (1 × ½in) piece of smoked salmon folded into three. Garnish with a tiny sprig of dill.

Toasties with Salmon Roe and Soured Cream

Makes 24 canapés

These little cases are brilliant for many canapés as they are both delicious, crisp, cheap and easy to make, as long as you have miniature tartlet tins.

6 or 7 slices white bread
melted unsalted butter
85ml/3fl oz soured cream
a little jar of salmon roe

Pre-heat oven to 200°/400°F/Gas Mark 6.

1   Cut the crusts off the bread and discard. Roll the bread as thinly as possible with a rolling pin. Brush with melted butter on both sides.

2   Cut tiny rounds out and put into a miniature pattie tin. Place another pattie tin on top to keep them in place.

3   Bake for 15 minutes.

4   When the toasties are cold, spoon or pipe a swirl of soured cream into each and top with some salmon roe.

Smoked Salmon Tartlets

Makes 24 canapés

If you can't afford caviare, use lumpfish roe (also known as mock caviare).

24 miniature shortcrust-pastry shells
55g/2oz smoked salmon
55ml/2fl oz soured cream
1 teaspoon chervil (optional), finely chopped
caviare (or lumpfish roe)

1   Slice the smoked salmon into very fine strips. Pipe a little soured cream (with the chervil, if using) into the pastry cases. Pile a little of the salmon julienne on top, and finish with a little caviare, positioned with the handle of a teaspoon.

Smoked Salmon and Quail's Egg Tartlets

Makes 24 canapés

A little finely chopped tarragon can be added to the mayonnaise if you wish. Remember that it has a very strong flavour though.

15g/½ oz smoked salmon
12 hard-boiled quails' eggs
mayonnaise (see page 120)
24 shortcrust pastry miniature tartlet cases

1   Slice the smoked salmon into a fine julienne. Halve the quails' eggs. Pipe a little mayonnaise into the pastry cases. Place the halved eggs, yolk-side up, on top. Place a few strips of smoked salmon on the top of each.

Fresh Salmon Croûtons

Makes 20 canapés; serves 4 or 5 as a starter

These little fried croûtons taste delectable, the marinade on the salmon being lemony and fresh. This also makes a good starter.

110g/4oz very fresh salmon, skinned
   and filleted
salt
4 teaspoons lemon juice

2 heaped tablespoons finely chopped
   shallot
3½ slices brown bread
olive oil

1   Remove the crusts from the bread and cut each slice into 6 3cm (1in) croûtons (and the half-slice into 3).

2   Slice the salmon into 20 thin medallions. These are far easier to cut using the thicker, upper fillet only.

3   Sprinkle with the lemon juice, 4 teaspoons of olive oil and the shallot. Leave to marinate for 1 hour.

4   When the salmon is ready, heat some oil in a frying pan. When it is just beginning to smoke put half the croûtons in. Turn over immediately. When golden brown on one side, turn them back and cook until crisp. Drain on absorbent paper, add more oil if necessary and repeat with the rest of the croûtons.

5   Cut the salmon into neat squares to fit the fried bread and serve immediately. If making them in advance, fried bread reheats very quickly in the oven with no ill-effects; the salmon can be drained from the marinade and kept in the fridge for a few hours without changing too much.

Herbed Salmon Delice

Makes 20 canapés

Another marinated raw salmon recipe. In this one the salmon is shown the marinade briefly, dredged in herbs then rolled up round a slice of lemon and secured with a cocktail stick. If you make your own flavoured oils, such as chilli or basil, try using these instead of the olive oil.

110g/4oz very fresh salmon fillet, skinned
2 lemons
1 tablespoon finely chopped chervil
1 tablespoon snipped chives
olive oil

1   If possible use only the upper, thicker section of the fillet. Cut into 20 wafer-thin slices. Otherwise, halve the fillet and slice the 2 portions into 10 medallions each. Needless to say the salmon must be very fresh and of good quality.

2   Cut the ends off 1 lemon. Stand on one end and with a sharp knife pare away the skin and all pith, sawing downwards with each cut. Slice the lemon flesh into 10 very thin slices and then halve each piece.

3   When you are ready to serve, place the salmon slices in a dish; squeeze the juice from one half of the second lemon into a measuring jug. Top up with oil, so that the mixture's proportions are one-third lemon to two-thirds oil.

4   Leave to marinate for about 5 minutes, until the salmon begins to lose its opaqueness and appears 'cooked'.

5   Drain from the liquid and press both sides of the fish pieces into the herbs. Place a piece of lemon on each.

6   Roll them up quite tightly, with the lemon on the inside, and skewer with a cocktail stick.

CHAPTER 7

SAUCES, STOCKS AND BUTTERS

Herb Sauce

Makes approx. 300ml/10fl oz; serves 6

This sauce is wickedly rich; the flour just stabilizes the cream, while the egg-yolks thicken it.

55g/2oz butter
2 shallots
1 teaspoon flour
2 tablespoons chopped parsley
2 tablespoons chopped tarragon
1 teaspoon French mustard

290ml/10fl oz double or whipping
 cream
2 egg-yolks
salt, black pepper
lemon juice

1   Sweat the finely chopped shallots in the butter until soft and translucent. Stir in the flour; cook for a few moments and then add the cream, mustard and plenty of black pepper. Allow the sauce to simmer gently for 10 minutes.

2   Stir a couple of spoons of the cream into the egg-yolks, then mix them back into the sauce. Stir gently over a low heat while the egg-yolks thicken the cream. Do not let the sauce boil.

3   Add the herbs; sharpen with the lemon juice and season with salt if necessary.

Clarified Butter

Makes 50g/just under 2oz

Clarified butter is used for sealing pâtés and for frying; I keep a jar permanently in the fridge. All recipes in this book that suggest frying in butter would benefit from the use of clarified butter. There are several ways of making clarified butter; this method is the easiest.

125g/4½ oz salted butter

1   Heat the butter in a small pan until it is foaming. Allow to settle for a few minutes. Remove scum from the surface of the butter, and then pour the remainder through a double layer of muslin or kitchen paper, stopping before you get to the milky residue at the bottom of the pan.

2   Use as required.

Beurre Montée

Makes approx. 300ml/10fl oz; serves 8

Beurre montée is a good sauce for those who don't want to run the risk of a butter and cream sauce that may curdle.

570ml/1 pint fish stock
140g/5oz chilled butter, cut into pieces
2 teaspoons flour
2 tablespoons double cream
1 tablespoon of any herb of your choice, finely chopped (for example tarragon, chervil or dill)
salt and black pepper

1   Boil the stock until reduced by half (down to 290ml/10fl oz).

2   Melt 30g (1oz) of the butter. Stir in the flour, cook for a few moments then remove from the heat. Pour in the reduced stock. Return to the heat and stir until boiling. Allow to simmer for a few minutes. Whisk in the remaining butter, piece by piece, over a very low heat. Add the cream and your chosen herb. Season to taste.

Hollandaise Sauce

Makes approx. 150ml/5fl oz; serves 4

Hollandaise must be the all-time favourite sauce to serve with salmon. It is the first to spring to mind and is loved by all.

2 egg-yolks
3 tablespoons white-wine vinegar
6 peppercorns
1 bay leaf
pinch of ground mace
110g/4oz butter, softened
salt, black pepper and lemon juice

---

1   Place the vinegar, mace, bay leaf and peppercorns in a small pan. Boil down to 1 tablespoon. Strain.

---

2   In a bowl set over hot but not simmering water, place the 2 egg-yolks and a piece of the butter. Cream them together, stirring constantly until they are just beginning to thicken.

---

3   Pour on the strained vinegar. Stirring all the time, start to add the butter, piece by piece, as the sauce slowly thickens. When all the butter is incorporated and the sauce is the consistency of thick yoghurt add salt, pepper, and a squeeze of lemon juice to sharpen the flavour.

---

4   You can keep the sauce warm for about 30 minutes: simply leave over the water, but off the heat and covered with a piece of buttered paper.

Bearnaise Sauce

Makes approx. 150ml/5fl oz; serves 4

Bearnaise is the herb-flavoured version of hollandaise sauce. Traditionally, it is meant for beef, but I find that salmon happily embraces the extra dimension that it offers.

3 tablespoons wine vinegar
1 bay leaf
1 shallot, finely chopped
1 tablespoon finely chopped
  tarragon, plus a sprig for the
  reduction

6 peppercorns
1 tablespoon finely chopped chervil
2 egg-yolks
110g/4oz softened butter
salt and pepper

1   Place the vinegar, the sprig of tarragon, the shallot, the bay leaf, and the peppercorns into a small pan. Boil until reduced down to 1 tablespoon. Strain.

2   In a bowl, set over hot but not simmering water, place the 2 egg-yolks and a piece of the butter. Cream them together, stirring constantly until they are just beginning to thicken.

3   Pour on the strained vinegar. Stirring all the time, start to add the butter, piece by piece, watching the sauce thicken slowly. When all the butter is incorporated and the sauce is the consistency of thick yoghurt, stir in the herbs and adjust the seasoning.

4   You can keep the sauce warm for about 30 minutes: simply leave over the water, but off the heat, and covered with a piece of buttered paper.

Beurre Blanc

Makes approx. 300ml/10fl oz; serves 6

Beurre blanc is my favourite classical sauce for fish. The buttery taste is complemented by the background of the vinegar reduction. It manages to taste rich without being cloying. I often serve it with a piece of plain poached haddock, spinach and new potatoes. Like this it both enhances and melds the flavours together.

225g/8oz unsalted butter (do not use
  salted)
1 shallot, finely chopped
6 peppercorns
1 bay leaf

3 tablespoons water
3 tablespoons vinegar
salt and pepper
lemon juice

1   Cut the butter into about 20 pieces; replace in the fridge as the butter must be very cold when used.

2   In a small saucepan, place the water, vinegar, peppercorns, bay leaf and shallot. Boil down to 2 tablespoons. Watch it very carefully, and if you are using a heavy-bottomed pan, remove from the heat before the reduction is complete as the heat will continue to evaporate the liquid.

3   Reduce the heat under the saucepan drastically. Add a lump of the butter and stir. When it has melted, quickly add another. Continue like this until all the butter has gone. Do not let the sauce come near to a simmer. If it does get too hot and starts to separate, add another piece of cold butter. The whole process should take about 5 minutes.

4   Add salt (very sparingly), pepper and lemon juice to taste.

Green Butter

Makes approx. 110g/4oz; serves 5

This is wonderful with fish cutlets, but also makes special-tasting baked potatoes and it is an unusual base to egg dishes such as scrambled egg.

110g/4oz butter, softened
½ bunch watercress

1 small bunch parsley
1 small bunch tarragon
1 shallot, finely chopped

1   Blanch the watercress and herbs for 30 seconds. Refresh in cold water, then squeeze in a cloth to make them as dry as possible. Chop to a very fine paste, or purée in a liquidizer.

2   Beat the butter until creamy. Mix everything together with the shallot. Wrap in cling-film and roll to a sausage shape.

3   Chill until needed, then slice into 10 pats.

Garlic and Lemon Butter

Makes 110g/4oz; serves 4

This butter is also delicious with steaks and lamb chops. If you intend to make it by hand rather than with a food-processor, use lemon zest instead of the juice which is difficult to incorporate manually.

110g/4oz butter, softened
2 large cloves garlic, crushed
juice of 1 lemon

1   Cream the butter in a food-processor. Add the garlic and lemon juice, and process again. Wrap in cling-film and roll to a sausage shape.

2   Chill. When ready to serve, slice into 10 pats.

Anchovy Butter

Makes 120g/4½oz; serves 5

The ancient Romans used a fermented fish product as a basic seasoning in much of their cooking. Anchovy is the nearest flavour we have to that now, and in small amounts it can enhance meat and vegetables dishes without making them taste fishy. This butter is a good way of incorporating the little amount needed and keeps for several weeks in the fridge. It is also divine on a plain grilled salmon steak!

1 tin anchovy fillets in oil
110g/4oz butter, softened
½ clove garlic
1 tablespoon finely chopped parsley (optional)

1   Beat the butter until creamy. Remove from the oil and finely mince the anchovy fillets. Beat into the butter (along with the parsley if wished). Alternatively, place everything in a food-processor and whizz until smooth.

2   Wrap in cling-film, roll into a sausage shape and chill. When you are ready to serve, slice into 10 small pats and place on the steaks. The butter will melt into the flesh imbuing it with a wonderful flavour.

Montpellier Butter

Makes 225g/9oz; serves 8

This old-fashioned 'butter' is perfect with salmon and quite unusual: it has a fuller flavour than the usual herb or 'green' butters. Don't be tempted to increase the seemingly small amounts of flavouring; they are just right.

15g/½ oz of each of the following:
  watercress
  parsley
  chervil
  tarragon
  chives
2 or 3 spinach leaves
1 level teaspoon finely minced
  shallot

½ gherkin, finely chopped
2 capers, finely chopped
1 anchovy fillet
yolk of a hard-boiled egg, crumbled
225g/8oz very soft butter
salt
cayenne pepper
olive oil

1   Blanch the herbs and spinach for 30 seconds. Drain; refresh in a bowl of cold water, drain again and squeeze in a cloth to remove as much water as possible.

2   Process until absolutely smooth. Turn into a bowl and cream in the butter a piece at a time. Beat in the crumbled egg-yolk, and stir in the gherkin, shallot and anchovy.

3   Let the butter down slightly with a little olive oil. Then season carefully with salt and cayenne.

4   Finally, rub the whole thing through a sieve; not all will go through. This makes enough to cover a 2.7kg (6lb) fish.

Mayonnaise

Makes approx. 300ml/10fl oz; serves 6

A home-made mayonnaise is incomparable to even the best of the commercial brands. It is satisfying to make and very easy, as long as you don't try to rush things.

2 egg-yolks
1 teaspoon mustard
150ml/5fl oz olive oil
150ml/5fl oz sunflower oil
1 tablespoon white-wine vinegar
lemon juice
salt and pepper

1   Put the yolks and the mustard in a bowl. Place the bowl on a damp cloth to prevent it slipping around. Beat the eggs together.

2   Using a teaspoon, add the oil, literally drop by drop, beating constantly. When you have incorporated half the oil, start to add the vinegar in small dribbles between the additions of oil. You will find that the mayonnaise will now take slightly larger drops of oil (up to half a teaspoon at the end).

3   Add seasoning and lemon juice to taste. If it is too thick for your liking add a little water.

If you have someone to help you, the time can be halved as one of you can drop in the oil while the other does the beating. Alternatively, you can use a food-processor or hand-mixer although I personally find that the results are heavier and with a slightly cooked taste. (If using a food-processor, don't be fooled by the speed of the blades into thinking you can add the oil much quicker – you can't, it simply conserves your energy!)

Aigrellette

Makes approx. 225ml/8fl oz; serves 5

This creamy-tasting sauce is ideal for anyone avoiding dairy products. Serve it cold, on poached salmon; or hot, by heating it gently in a bain-marie, for any salmon plainly baked, grilled or fried. It is perfect.

1 egg-yolk
pinch of mustard powder
4 tablespoons olive oil
4 tablespoons sunflower oil
1 tablespoon white-wine vinegar

85ml/3fl oz fish stock
1 tablespoon chopped tarragon
1 tablespoon chopped chives
1 tablespoon chopped chervil
salt and pepper

1   Put the egg-yolk in a bowl with the mustard. Stand the bowl on a damp cloth to prevent it sliding around.

2   Mix the oils together. With a wooden spoon in one hand and oil in the other, add the oil to the egg-yolk, literally drop by drop, beating all the time as you would for mayonnaise.

3   When half the oil has been incorporated, start to let the emulsion down, a little at a time with the stock and vinegar. It should be the consistency of single cream. Finally, stir in the herbs and adjust the seasoning.

Grellette Sauce

Makes approx. 150ml/5fl oz; serves 4

This unusual sauce is wonderfully fresh and pure-tasting. It would make a good dressing if you wanted something to combine well with salmon and a salad. I serve it instead of mayonnaise with cold lobster.

3 large tomatoes
3 tablespoons double cream
1 teaspoon white-wine vinegar
1 teaspoon Dijon mustard
10 tarragon leaves, finely chopped

1 tablespoon finely chopped parsley
1 teaspoon finely chopped chervil
1 teaspoon cognac
salt and cayenne pepper

1   Skin and halve the tomatoes. Discard the pips. Cut 1 tomato into neat cubes. Salt it and leave to drain in a sieve. Chop the other 2 tomatoes to a fine purée. Salt these and leave to drain also.

2   Whisk the cream until thick, with the cayenne, some salt, the cognac, mustard and the vinegar. Stop immediately if it looks as if it is going to separate. Stir in the herbs and tomato purée. Finally, fold in the cubed tomato and adjust the seasoning. Chill before serving.

Walnut and Horseradish Sauce

Makes approx. 500ml/18fl oz; serves 6

Horseradish makes a popular, if surprising, partner to fish in many sauces. I love this one because I'm fond of walnuts, but also the texture is pleasing when married to the tender flakes of a cold poached salmon.

140g/5oz shelled walnuts
140g/5oz grated horseradish,
  (prepared grated horseradish
  sold in jars will do)
7g/¼ oz sugar

squeeze of lemon
30g/1oz breadcrumbs
290ml/10fl oz double cream
salt

1   Pour boiling water over the walnuts. Leave for a few minutes, then drain well and put into a clean tea-towel. Rub the nuts vigorously to remove the dark and bitter skin.

2   Chop them finely and place in a bowl with the sugar, breadcrumbs, cream, and salt. Add the horseradish until you feel it is in balance with the sauce. Adjust the flavour with lemon juice and more salt if necessary.

Dill and Mustard Sauce

Makes approx. 85ml/3fl oz; serves 5

This is the classic sauce for gravad lax. It will keep for several days in the fridge.

4 tablespoons olive oil
1 tablespoon white-wine vinegar
1 tablespoon Dijon mustard

1 tablespoon chopped dill
2 teaspoons sugar
salt and pepper

1   Combine all the ingredients except the oil in a bowl. Add the oil drop by drop, whisking vigorously. Place in the fridge until required.

Fish Stock and Court Bouillon

Makes approx. 1 1/2pt

Use these recipes for the poaching of any fish and for countless good sauces. Unlike meat stocks they can be prepared very quickly and are well worth the effort. Court bouillon and stock are made in an identical manner, the only difference being that the latter includes fish skin and bones. The skin and bones should be of white fish, such as whiting, plaice, cod or sole, rather than from salmon (which gives a slightly oily liquor). Do not worry if only salmon is available: just avoid using the skin. The court bouillon is an aromatic liquor that can be used either for delicate sauces – where too fishy a taste would be undesirable – or as a substitute for fish stock. Any left-over stock or court bouillon can be poured into ice-trays and frozen: these individual stock cubes are very useful, especially for recipes that call for only a small amount. Once frozen, the cubes can be transferred to a plastic bag to free the ice-trays for other uses.

For court bouillon and fish stock:
1 litre/2 pints water
1 slice of lemon or a splash of
   white wine
parsley stalks
1 bay leaf
½ onion, sliced

½ carrot, sliced
½ stick celery, sliced
pinch of salt
12 peppercorns

For fish stock only:
500g/1lb white-fish skin and bones
   (or salmon bones)

For both recipes:

1   Place all the ingredients except the fish bones into a large saucepan and bring to the boil. Simmer for 30 minutes.

2   For the fish stock: add the fish to the pan and simmer for another 25 minutes. Never cook fish bones for longer, or the stock may gain a bitter taint.

3   If you like, you can strain the stock or court bouillon, then bring back to a rolling boil and reduce by half. When it is cool, pour into ice trays and freeze.

APPENDIX

To help you get more out of the book and to organise your menus, here are a few suggestions for various types of meal or event.

LOW FAT

*Salmon Alexander	38
Salmon Terrine with Vegetables	82
Poached Salmon	12
Marinated Salmon I	92
*Baked Steaks in Foil	21

(*denotes that leaving the butter out of the recipe will have no adverse effect.)

FAMILY SUPPERS

Soured Cream Salmon Pie	51
Salmon Mornay	65
Salmon Baked with Cucumber	15
Salmon Fishcakes	79
Salmon Cutlets	63

STARTERS

Pot-Pourri Parcels	26
Plaited Salmon With Beurre Montée	40
Salmon Soufflé	70
Spinach and Salmon Roulade	97
Potted Salmon	74

FISH COURSES

Salmon Steaks in Newspaper	24
Brochettes of Salmon and Scallops	28
Salmon and Sorrel Steaks	35
Salmon Feuillettes with Spinach	60
Marinated Salmon II and Melon Salad	93

MAIN COURSES FOR DINNER PARTIES

Salmon Cooked in Champagne	37
Salmon Steaks in Cream	34
Salmon en Croûte	46
Salmon in Filo Pastry with Watercress Mousseline	54
Salmon with Roquefort Sauce	42

BRUNCH

Salmon Kedgeree	67
Salmon Roe with Eggs	66
Salmon Pojarski	64
Salmon Quiche	45
Individual Salmon Filo Koulibiacs	56

LUNCHES

Smoked Salmon and Scrambled Eggs	84
Salmon Soup	78
Torte de Saumon	59
Smoked Salmon and Herb Salad	89
Grilled Salmon with Flavoured Butters	22

INDEX